"The Greatest War Story of All – Takes rank with 'All Quiet on the Western Front'. She fulfilled in every respect the conditions which made the terrible profession of a spy dignified and honourable. Dwelling behind the German line within sound of cannon, she continually obtained and sent information of the highest importance to the British Intelligence Authorities. Her tale is a thrilling one ... the main description of her life and intrigues and adventures is undoubtedly authentic. I was unable to stop reading it until 4 a.m."

—Winston Churchill 1932

I WAS A SPY!

I WAS A SPY!

The Classic Account of Behind-the-Lines Espionage in the First World War

BY
MARTHE McKENNA

FOREWORD BY
THE RT. HON. WINSTON S. CHURCHILL P.C., C.H., M.P.
(*Secretary of State for War, 1918–1921*)

POOLOFLONDON

First published in 1932

This edition published in Great Britain in 2015 by
The Pool of London Press
A Division of Casemate Publishers
10 Hythe Bridge Street
Oxford OX1 2EW, UK
and
908 Darby Road, Havertown, PA 19083, USA

www.pooloflondon.com

Text © Marthe McKenna
Volume © The Pool of London Press 2015

A CIP record for this book is available from the British Library

Hardcover edition: ISBN 978-1-910860-03-8
Ebook edition: ISBN 978-1-910860-04-5

Printed in the Czech Republic by FINIDR s.r.o..

To receive regular email updates on forthcoming Pool of London titles,
email info@pooloflondon.com with Pool of London Updates in the subject
field.

For a complete list of Pool of London Press and Casemate titles, please contact:
CASEMATE PUBLISHERS (UK)
Telephone (01865) 241249
Fax (01865) 794449
Email: casemate-uk@casematepublishers.co.uk
www.casematepublishers.co.uk

CASEMATE PUBLISHERS (US)
Telephone (610) 853-9131
Fax (610) 853-9146
Email: casemate@casematepublishing.com
www.casematepublishing.com

FOREWORD

BY THE RT. HON. WINSTON S. CHURCHILL, P.C., C.H., M.P.
(*Secretary of State for War, 1918–1921*)

Self-preservation has forced States and armies in every age to exact the penalty of death from a spy. The elaborate deceit which is the essence of espionage also casts its slur upon those who undertake it.

Nevertheless, a Secret Service agent who is not actuated by any sordid motive, but inspired by patriotism, and ready to pay the well-known forfeit, deserves respect and honour from those he serves so faithfully.

The courage of a soldier advancing in a forlorn hope is not greater, and his ordeal is far less trying, than that of the man—or woman—who, sometimes for years, dwells in the midst of the enemy with his life hanging upon every chance word or action.

The fortitude required for the endurance of these prolonged strains is equal to anything demanded of the bravest fighting troops, and the services which can be rendered to King and Country may sometimes far exceed in importance the results of the most splendid acts of devotion in the field.

Many were the dauntless and devoted people who sacrificed their lives unhonoured and unsung for the Allied cause.

It is often the fashion of our countrymen to belittle their own efficiency in matters of this kind, and to exult the superior craft and ability of foreigners.

But I believe it to be unquestionably true that the British Secret Service before and during the Great War was more skilfully organized, more daringly pursued and achieved more important results than that of any other country, friend or foe.

Martha McKenna, the heroine of this account, fulfilled in every respect the conditions which make the terrible profession of a spy dignified and honourable.

Dwelling behind the German line, within sound of the cannon, she continually obtained and sent information of the highest importance to the British Intelligence authorities.

She reported the movement of troops; she destroyed, or endeavoured to destroy, ammunition dumps; she assisted the escape of British prisoners; she directed the British aeroplanes where to strike at the billets, camps, and assemblies of the German troops, and thus brought death upon hundreds of the enemies and oppressors of her country.

In the meanwhile she worked in the German hospitals, rendering the merciful and tender service of a nurse to those upon whom, in another capacity, she sought to bring death and ruin, and for that service she was actually awarded the German Iron Cross in the early days of the War.

She holds the French and Belgian decorations for distinguished gallantry. She was mentioned in Sir Douglas Haig's dispatches of the 8th November, 1918, "for gallant and distinguished service in the field," and it was my duty as Secretary of State for War formally to convey to her in 1919 the appreciation of his Majesty.

Her tale is a thrilling one. Having begun it, I could not put out my light till four o'clock in the morning.

I cannot, of course, vouch for the accuracy of every incident; but the main description of her life, intrigues, and adventures is undoubtedly authentic.

She was caught at last by a clever trap following upon a tiny accident.

By all the laws of war her life was forfeit. She did not dispute the justice of her fate.

It was a merciful act to commute her sentence into life imprisonment, which, in the nature of things, would probably not last longer than the duration of the War.

We have now reached again that memorable week in the year when all our thoughts go back to the stirring hours of August 1914, when Britain and her Empire drew, in the name of honour and humanity, the sword which was not to be sheathed until absolute victory had been won.

Such a tale as this may well revive the sacrifices and hazards of the Great War, although its bitterness has faded, as it ought to fade, with time.

EDITOR'S NOTE

It was a clear sunny day of blue skies in the summer of 1931 when I left Thourout during a walking tour across Belgium. I intended to find lodging for that night in Langemarck. About three o'clock in the afternoon I noticed the wind whistling in the tree-tops. It struck you in the face with a chill, menacing blast on the rising ground. The sky turned suddenly black. The atmosphere was leaden when the thunder bellowed, then the rain began to whisper in the dust. Before long it fell in hissing torrents, and I fled for the gloomy shelter of a clump of trees.

Then I saw the figure of a man struggling along the road from the way I had come. . . . He joined me under the trees, nodded and lit a pipe. There was nothing to note about him except that he was of good class, and rather wetter than I was. I addressed him in bad French.

"I'm English," he smiled, "although it's quite possible I look a trifle Flemish. I've lived in this country for twelve years now, you see."—That was how I met Mr. McKenna. As the storm showed no sign of abating he invited me to stay the night at Westroosebeke.

9

We entered a picturesque but new-looking village of red brick.

"This place was a heap of rubbish in 1919," commented my companion, "but it seemed to grow up like mushrooms overnight."

Presently, waterlogged and muddy, I was greeted by a quiet Belgian lady in the spacious hall of a gabled house, standing in the depths of a garden scented with damp flowers.

It was a chance remark of mine after dinner which brought me the astonishing information that my hostess had been a spy for the British during the War, that she had been court-martialled and condemned to death—and how it was that she came to be still alive. I insisted that she ought to write her strange story, and I naturally wanted her to write it in English. She replied that that would be very hard. I begged her to let me edit it for her and to this she agreed.

"Because I am a woman I could not serve my country as a soldier. I took the only course open to me.—And let it be remembered by those who disdain the spy, that in every case where I played with another's life, I was also playing with my own!—I want to put that in front of my Memoirs," said Mrs. McKenna.

She wishes to dedicate her book to the women of all nations, friend and foe, who died, who strove actively, and who suffered during the War of 1914–1918.

For certain photographs which Mrs. McKenna was unable to provide, I am indebted to the authorities of the Imperial War Museum, South Kensington.

E. E. P. Tisdall

I WAS A SPY!

CHAPTER I

On the night of the 2nd of August, 1914, my father burst into the kitchen of our old farmhouse at Westroosebeke. We stopped talking involuntarily when we saw his face.

"The Germans have invaded Belgium," he breathed; "King Albert has ordered general mobilization. The boys will have to make for their depôts by the first train. It is terrible. Our troops are massing on Liège and Namur. God knows what will happen! Belgium can never hold up the German hordes."

My mother finished ironing a lace cap, put it carefully to one side and smiled anxiously at him.

"Martha," she addressed me over her shoulder, "go out and bring the boys in and tell them what has happened." And then to my father: "Do not worry, Felix; France will account for these Boches. Soon French soldiers will be fighting shoulder to shoulder with our own. Come now, take off your heavy boots. Supper is almost ready."

That was how we heard of the Great War at Westroosebeke. Most of us were incapable of realizing the real seriousness of the calamity. Only a few days earlier people had been flocking into Westroosebeke from far and near for the annual village

Kermis. The church bells pealed out merrily, little chapels gay with flowers stood along the roadways, the roundabouts in the teeming market-square blared an endless tune which mingled with the bellowing of the hucksters and showmen at their stalls, and everywhere old friends were making the most of reunions. Omer, my eldest brother, had just come back from his term of military service, so it was a special time of rejoicing for us.

Day by day rumour swept through the country towns of Flanders. Then there came that distant roll of gun-fire, and sudden flashes would flicker across the skyline of nights. Our troops were falling back. Liège had fallen, its dozen forts pounded to dust beneath the ruthless iron heel of Ludendorff. Namur, held by our men till the last, had also crumbled to a heap of jagged stone and scrap-iron. Every morning we learned that the relentless grey wave had come closer, and there we remained, stunned, unable to believe that one day we should see men in spiked helmets in the village street.

One day a little donkey-cart piled high with mattresses and bundles, accompanied by a tall young peasant woman, with two little children who trotted at her heels, halted in the roadway outside our house.

Her lips were tightly set and she held a far-away look in her eyes as she leaned over the gate.

"Have you any food you can spare for the children, please? Perhaps I could do some work for you in payment for the food."

I brought the little family into the kitchen, where my mother attended to them. The young mother had heard nothing of her husband since the day he hurried to join his regiment. Their village had been shelled out of existence; she and her children had walked for three days; she had no more money to buy food. They had heard they would find shelter and rations at Ypres. There were thousands more like them, and even now they were pouring through the village street. Later, when I went shopping, the entire roadway was blocked with creaking carts, sweating animals and weary dust-smothered human beings. Animals were eating the hedges and the grass in the front gardens unchecked. One horse lay dead in the shafts, and the owner, a young, well-dressed woman, sat on the step sobbing bitterly. Her husband was dead, her home razed to the ground, she had lost her little son in the mêlée, and was penniless. The children hopped in and out cheerfully, nothing daunted by their plight; but bravest were the old white-haired men and women, many of them lying sick on their bundles. Vituperatively they cursed the invaders, but they looked upon all that happened with philosophical eyes.

The stream of refugees seemed never-ending. Westroosebeke became a huge temporary camp. As can be understood many were starving, but the houses in the village were rarely broken into. Our house, barns and outhouses were packed with unfortunates, as were all the other houses. Old people died and were hastily buried, and their relations passed on. Small children were making their way across country by themselves. One day three stragglers, cut off from the Army, limped into Westroosebeke. It was our first sight of men who had emerged from the flaming furnace. In their eyes was the look of wild beasts; filthy, unshaven, their tattered uniforms streaked with blood and dirt, their blistered feet bursting through their boots, fatigue had turned their speech to an incoherent babble. Then the sky darkened, and the rain hissed down on the turmoil; but the long procession walked on doggedly through the mire, often at nights sleeping in the sticky, saturated pastures.

One sunny morning a fierce rushing noise roared to a shrieking crescendo overhead. There came a crashing detonation in the village street. Silence for a moment as the mushroom-cloud of black smoke cleared and debris pattered to the ground. Then rose cries as of animals in pain, as women and children stirred feebly amid pools of blood in the roadway. Strange moustached cavalry in flat round caps and mustard-coloured uniforms rode into Westroosebeke. The British were coming, flew the rumour from mouth to mouth. These men were kindly and tried to help the refugees. But they soon mounted and rode away. Shells dropped now and again, but the village was obviously not as yet a mark for the German guns.

Many of the villagers joined the stream of fugitives. There were moments when this heartrending exeunt was fraught with a grim humour. Harry Verstele, village wit and wagon-maker, had just been married. When a shell landed on his little workshop he decided the time had come to go, and carry his bride with him. Not being in possession of a horse as yet, he wheeled out his largest wheelbarrow. Instead of filling this with the bare necessities he piled his choicest pieces of furniture on it. "No plundering swine is going to pig it in Germany with my best furniture," he growled; "nor in my best clothes either!" Harry's savings had bought for him a beautiful shiny top-hat, a long-tail coat, cuffs, dickey and patent buttoned shoes, and his bride had a very fine wedding-gown for a peasant girl. So Harry and his better half departed that evening with the stream in all the glory of full wedding regalia, wheeling their barrow before them!

Two squadrons of French cavalry reined up in a cloud of dust soon after the departure of the British, and since our house was on a hill outside the village with a commanding outlook over the flat sweep of countryside which we now scanned for a sight of the dreaded Germans, the officers were soon examining our buildings critically.

"I advise you to go, Mademoiselle," a lieutenant advised me hurriedly. "It is but a moment and our mitrailleuse will be here. We cannot hope to stop these bloody Boches for long. We are but a remnant!"

Little sweating blue-clad cavalrymen overran the premises, while my father and our man—who was over military age—led the exhausted horses to the trough in the yard. Everywhere resounded the sound of hammering and the crash of masonry. They were knocking out loopholes in the walls which faced towards the enemy, and barricading the windows with furniture, sacks of earth and anything they could lay hands on. Spent bullets began to whistle outside. I felt terribly frightened, but also terribly interested. From an upper window I could see dark masses steadily moving in the direction of Westroosebeke. Suddenly the pulsing rattle of *mitrailleuse* broke out below. German bullets flattened against the walls thick and fast now, or ricochetted mournfully into the fields. Two clean bullet holes showed in the pane an inch above my head.

"Martha, come down into the cellar!" cried my mother. "Quickly, now, and bring what food you can." But I crouched fascinated at a corner of the window. Groups of grey men in spiked helmets were running towards the village. I could almost see the strained looks on their white faces. Behind moved solid grey masses. Here and there men fell sprawling in the dust as fire of the *mitrailleuse* caught them. I remember thinking of autumn leaves swept by the wind. Some lay twitching, some dragged themselves to the rear, but the others came on without looking. Cattle galloped wild between the houses, and all the while the shells shrieked overhead; and out of the smoke and dust rising from Westroosebeke sounded the roar of tumbling masonry.

At last I dragged myself from that window. Momentarily the Germans were held up. At the foot of the stairs, deathly pale, retching fearfully, a French soldier sat rocking himself to and fro and clutching his stomach from which the blood spurted. Although I had been partially trained as a doctor, and was on my second vacation when the War broke out, I found myself trembling at the knees and a sick feeling rose inside me. The man had not long to live. His agonized eye met mine—"Water," he mouthed; but I knew that would only increase his sufferings. I propped his back against the wall, urged him to keep still, then as I could do no more joined my parents in the cellar.

Overhead roared the chorus of *mitrailleuse* like a battery of pneumatic drills, and now and then rang out an order or a scream of pain. There in the darkness, holding my mother's hand and listening to father and our old friend Lucelle Deldonck whispering together, little did I imagine that in a short while I should be an agent in the service of the British.

"Courage," said my father, as a shell burst over the roof, bringing down slates and mortar with a crash, "the French will beat them back."

He knew it was not true. So did we all. Nothing could stay for long the rushing torrent of that impetuous grey wave. We seemed to wait in that cellar for years, shaking with the terror of the unknown. Already we had heard terrible tales of what had happened in other villages. One girl, driven crazy, had hurled herself from a top window, and there were many such other tales. And yet I could hardly realize that what was happening around us was reality.

The *mitrailleuse* overhead ceased firing; sharp orders; a clattering of heavy boots; then silence—broken only by faint moans. I crept up the cellar steps. The French had gone, leaving their dead and seriously wounded in the hall, which glistened with wet blood like a shambles. Occasional firing still sounded outside but it was becoming distant. I ran to one of the barricaded windows in the front parlour and peered through a cranny. Groups of Germans with rifles slung over their shoulders were wearily making their way into Westroosebeke. I remember looking at my wrist-watch. It was just two o'clock in the afternoon, and I wondered in a detached way what my fate was going to be.

The kitchen door was thrust violently open. I knew the German language well, so pulling myself together I went to face the worst. Standing in the open doorway and glancing suspiciously around stood a young German officer, dirty and dishevelled. Behind him shone the bayonets of a platoon of troops. When he saw he was faced by a woman, he slipped his revolver into its holster and wiped the beads of sweat off his forehead.

"N'y-a-t-il pas de gens dans cette maison que vous?" he rapped, stamping into the centre of the room. A sergeant, a corporal and a section of soldiers entered, the others sat down outside on the ground and began to smoke.

"My father, my mother, and a friend are sheltering in the cellar," I told him in German.

"The walls of this house are loopholed. Your father is a civilian sharpshooter. You know the penalty for that, eh? Bring them up, corporal."

"My father is an old man. He has not fired a shot against you. It was French soldiers only who were shooting from here——"

"I have heard that story too many times before. This is not the first village we have entered. Fourteen of my men are casualties and fire coming from this house was responsible. If those who were with him have run away, your father can suffer alone."

My father, mother and Lucelle were dragged into the kitchen by the Gefreiter (corporal) and his men. My mother was on the point of fainting. Lucelle jerked herself free from the soldiers, and with her white hair dangling over her face and fists clenched glared at the young officer in defiance. My father was still smoking his pipe.

"Take that damned pipe out of your mouth," roared the Feldwebel (sergeant); and one of the soldiers seized it out of his mouth, knocked out the ash on his boot and pocketed it with a chuckle.

"Old man, you are a sharpshooter," accused the officer.

My father shook his head helplessly. My mother gave a low wail.

"Be merciful," I pleaded. "You have no proof."

"Silence," he shouted. "Do not argue. This place has been a nest of sharpshooters. It must be burnt down. Feldwebel, see to this immediately." He turned on my father and his lips snapped tight. "As for you, old man, you can bake in your own oven! Gefreiter, lock him in the cellar." The corporal caught my father by the collar and kicked him down the steps and spat after him.

"Filthy sharpshooter," he growled, slamming the door. I rushed to help my mother who had collapsed.

"You infernal butchers," hissed my aunt.

"Be quiet, Mademoiselle, this sharpshooting has got to be put an end to——"

He tipped his helmet to the back of his head, then took out a cigarette and lit it. The men outside had gathered at the door watching. There was a wild light in their eyes and some of them were grinning.

"Gretchen," snapped the officer turning on a dirty bearded soldier with a bloody bandage on his left hand, "collect all the food you can find in the house. I, for one, am hungry; and what about you, my friends?" His disreputable troops stiffened for a moment and let out a chorus of assent. Then they sprang back as a tall fiercely moustached Hauptmann (captain) strided into the kitchen.

"Hullo, Von Roone," he smiled, touching his helmet in answer to the lieutenant's smashing salute.

"Caught a sharpshooter here, sir."

"Well, I can leave you to deal with that situation. By the way, if you take any food from this place make some Belgian taste it before you touch it. More likely than not it will be poisoned. Hellish funny sight I saw in the street just now. Comic old woman who owned a café. Company halts outside. Officers go in.

"'Here, Mother, you drink first,' roars the Hauptmann breaking off the neck of a bottle and pushing it towards her. 'No poison for me to-day, thank you!' Lieutenants copy Hauptmann—Ober Feldwebel copies lieutenants—Feldwebels come next—Gefreiters follow—old dame doing a non-stop 'booze,' empty bottles beginning to pile up—naturally the privates queue up and follow everybody else—men of another company join the end of the queue—old girl staggering around quite 'blind' last I saw of her—die or burst in the end!"

The Hauptmann's eyes turned upon us.

"You can turn the women loose," he said, and marched out into the yard. The Feldwebel and two privates entered the kitchen door at that moment. They were carrying our drums of household oil, and immediately began to spill the oil over furniture and woodwork.

"We've already saturated the other rooms downstairs, sir."

"Good, Feldwebel, in that case the bonfire may as well start." Then he addressed us. "I will give you five minutes to collect any personal belongs you may want. I don't care what you do in the village, but do not try to leave it on any account or there will be trouble."

Dazedly we flung together a few belongings under the eye of the Gefreiter who, I must admit, helped us to support my mother and carry our bundles. Then we found ourselves standing huddled, dry-eyed, out in the highway, gazing fearfully back at the house where my father lay a helpless prisoner in the cellar.

Suddenly a puff of white smoke billowed out from the kitchen window. Shouts came from the house. Thick smoke belched from every lower window, and then fierce red tongues began to lick upward. We stared fascinated till my mother gave a moan like an animal in pain, then we slowly walked into Westroosebeke.

We passed two men of the village and one woman sprawled face downward in the dust—dead. Long grey columns of troops were swinging through Westroosebeke singing with coarse, harsh voices. The troops of the erstwhile first line they were passing through were bivouacked along the sides of the streets up against the houses. All the cafés were crammed to the doors, and cheers, laughter and stray words of obscene songs floated out. Every now and again a hiccuping soldier staggered blindly down the street amid the jibes of his fellows. The few officers we passed standing about seemed to take little notice of such conduct. Many of the troops I saw were mere boys and most of these lay stretched at full length utterly worn out.

In the centre of the village they had collected all the wounded. It was terrible; the roadway was soaked in blood. Doctors and orderlies with brows dripping and sleeves rolled up bent continuously among those writhing, groaning, red-bespattered forms. Lying in a little group by themselves were French soldiers, and the injured men and women of our village. These were receiving no attention at all, for the German medical staff were too much occupied with their own wounded. There, among those pinched faces in the little group of our own wounded, I recognized several neighbours, and was running forward to see what I could do to help them, when two German stretcher-bearers told me roughly to get about my business.

As we went on, a red-faced, gross-looking soldier, badly intoxicated, meandered up the street, brandishing his rifle aimlessly about his head and intoning to himself. Suddenly it seemed as though a horse had kicked my elbow, and instantaneously a sharp report almost deafened me in one ear. I saw the blood trickling down my arm and splashing over my dress, but somehow I felt no pain. Either on purpose or through carelessness that drunken German had fired off the round in his breech. For a moment he swayed staring at me with startled eyes, then when he found I did not fall dead, he gave a yell of laughter, and shambled on his way.

We intended to seek shelter with M. Hoot, an old friend of my father, who owned a large house in the village. We had not time to tap on the door before it was opened and my father stood before us. We could not believe our eyes. My mother rushed to him. He pulled us inside and closed the door. He had managed to tear away the bricks surrounding the airvent from the cellar, and so escape, while the lieutenant and his men were watching on the other side of our burning home. For a moment we were all four of us hilarious, joking in forgetfulness of what was happening around us, but the voices of a German battalion singing as they marched, quickly brought us to earth, and we went into the kitchen where M. and Mme. Hoot greeted us sympathetically. Several other neighbours were collected, and there we sat with scarce a whisper, disturbed only by the noise of activity, until darkness fell.

M. Hoot rose and took his pipe from his mouth. "We have had no food since early this morning," he said. "Probably it is the same with you. There is none here. Those bloody Boches ransacked the house when they first entered Westroosebeke. But I am going to get food somehow. I shall go alone, as it is safer." Paying no heed to his wife's terrified remonstrances he slipped out into the night.

It seemed that he was gone for centuries as we sat in the dark kitchen, illuminated only by faint white light which filtered through the mullioned window from the moonlight outside. I could hear Mme. Hoot sobbing quietly to herself. Suddenly there was a rustle behind us and a voice whispered, "Well, my friends, I have got some meat, and plenty of it. You can eat your fill. Now draw the curtains and get the fire lighted quickly." M. Hoot lit a candle. That sleek well-brushed citizen whom I used often to visit with my mother, looked indeed an uncouth figure as he posed in the candlelight, his good clothes crumpled and muddy, his damp hair half hiding triumphant eyes, as he raised aloft a huge hunk of meat from a bloodstained newspaper. "A fine joint, eh—I cut it from a dead horse," he almost laughed as he wiped stains of the post-mortem from his face with his handkerchief.

It seemed that we had not eaten for days, our mouths began to water at the savoury scent of cooking. Then, without one word of warning, there came a crash of rifle butts on the door, the windows suddenly shattered inwards, and the outline of spiked helmets showed in the moonlight. The house was full of trampling boots and shouting voices.

"To the cellar, run," yelled M. Hoot, seizing his wife and rushing her into the passage. Breathless, terrified we piled down the cellar steps. The ray of an electric-torch pierced the blackness, and to my amazement I saw that the place was already full of cowering refugees. Overhead footsteps thundered, then the door at the top of the cellar steps flew open and a German stood in the aperture waving a lantern. Shrieking oaths he deliberately emptied the magazine of his rifle into the living blackness below. The succeeding crashes in that confined space seemed like earth-shaking detonations. Bullets whizzed and ricochetted from steps to wall and back again. Wild screams rang out, then cries of pain. Three men were hit. Fortunately most of the bullets lodged in a vat of butter.

The German came lurching down the steps and others followed. Some of our men were for fighting and in the momentary mêlée the lantern was extinguished. An officer was roaring orders from the top of the steps and then we were being urged up at the point of bayonets. I do not know whether the deed was done purposely, but when one of the soldiers emerged into the light of the passage, a tiny baby was spitted on the point of his bayonet. Drawing off the feebly twitching body, with an oath he threw it into the arms of the nearest woman. It was the young mother. She let out one ghastly scream which I shall never forget and fell senseless to the floor.

They lined us up in the moonlight, almost fifty silent, resigned prisoners. No words of parting were allowed, but presently the men were disappearing into the shadows under escort, and we women and children were hustled back into the cellar.

It was not until several hours later that we discovered that Lucelle was missing. Had she been killed and was her body lying in the garden or in some ditch, or had she successfully made her escape in the confusion? We knew her for an active determined woman, but of course dare not inquire of the Germans, and her disappearance remained a mystery which often troubled us.

There, for fourteen days, we remained prisoners, allowed out but once a day to procure food and water. Little air leaked into that cellar and after a short time the atmosphere had grown thick and foul. It was damp down there, and to those of us who had no bedding the nights were cruelly cold, as we were not allowed sufficient fuel to keep alight at nights the small fire we lit in the middle of the floor in the daytime. The German authorities seemed to have forgotten about us. We were given insufficient water; the cellar was never cleaned; and no kind of sanitary arrangements were made.

Then, one morning, we were ordered up from the cellar and told by a staff officer that we might proceed to our homes, but that we must behave ourselves. The men had also been released; and that afternoon my father rejoined us. His experiences had been similar to our own. We got lodgings in a neighbour's house.

Westroosebeke had now become a rest billet and medical clearing-station behind the line. After the mad fever-pitch excitement of their first days of war, the Germans seemed to have quietened. They regarded us sternly, but there was no ill-treatment and no longer any disorderly scenes in the streets.

I heard that three nuns had brought their aged poor from shell-swept Passchendaele and had taken the large house across the street. They turned it into an emergency hospital, treating both German wounded and wounded Allied prisoners, so I went across to offer my assistance.

"God has sent you," said the Mother Superior, when I told her I was a trained nurse. "Come with me—I will show you. Be brave, my daughter."

Inside the house men with open gangrenous wounds, men armless, legless, blind, lay tossing on beds, on sofas, on the floor, while a single doctor with infinitely tired eyes and two German orderlies moved among them. The doctor only came for certain hours each day, and we had to make shift with the two orderlies. The Germans gave us drugs and bandages, and although they were always willing to do their best for enemy wounded, they naturally attended to their own men first, and these were so numerous that they very often had no time for the others. All the wounded, friend or foe, were touchingly appreciative of our aid; we did duty twenty hours out of the twenty-four, and I believe much misery and agony was alleviated by our efforts.

One morning I opened the front door to a German staff officer followed by a smart N.C.O.

"Where is the Mother Superior, Fräulein?" he demanded. "You have been seen to show lights from the upper windows at night."

I assured him that it was entirely unintentional, but it was useless. He said spies were at work in the district. The three nuns came down and he interviewed them searchingly, while the N.C.O. stood like a ramrod in the background. "You will pack your things and leave for Courtrai within three hours," he ordered them. "Otherwise you will be liable to arrest. You,

Fräulein, will stay here. You are an excellent interpreter and your medical knowledge has been much appreciated."

And so the good nuns hired a cart, loaded up their bundles, and departed in tears along the road to Courtrai; and I remained alone among those men of another nation to help the wounded.

Everyone was suspected by the Germans of being a spy. Even smoke rising from a chimney might be construed as cunning smoke signals. All went in fear for their lives. The aged priest of Staden was accused of showing lights from his church tower, and without any court-martial, or reference to higher authority, was dragged out into the fields, handed a spade to dig his own grave, and then shot into it. Spy mania was soon fanned into a flame. Two elderly workmen were shot out of hand because they had offered to water German horses; it being thought that they intended to poison them; and their corpses were left crumpled by the roadside as a warning. Every civilian remaining in Westroosebeke (and by the beginning of December there were only twelve of us women who lodged together in one house) was interrogated closely by agents. Two sentries were sent to mount guard over our house and generally keep us under observation. I worked at the hospital and as an interpreter, and as a rule found myself treated with much deference; the others did washing for the officers and any various odd jobs which were allotted to them.

The authorities ordered that the eleven women should move further behind the line as they were suspected of spying. Once more I was permitted to stay because of my usefulness, and as several Germans with whom I had become acquainted disliked losing the women who had washed and darned and generally looked after them, they decided to send me over to H.Q. at Hooglede, with a letter praising our good services and requesting that all might remain. The permission was granted, and I walked back to Westroosebeke with my soldier guard. Arrived at the house I found that by order of the local military police my mother and the other women had already gone. I was alone in the house with two tough-looking German guards. That night I did not dare to go to bed.

The two soldiers sat with their tunics unbuttoned by the kitchen fire.

"Come, Fräulein," rasped the elder, a gross fellow, taking his curly pipe from his lips. "Drink with us to the success of Germany."

Smirking foolishly he handed me a glass of schnapps, and when I would not drink, swallowed it himself and poured out some more. The other man was lank and cadaverous with a spotty face. He had spent the whole evening leering disgustingly at me. Presently they grew drunk and began to argue with each other. I edged towards the door. The lank man stopped talking, for he had seen me out of the corner of his eye. He jumped up, caught me and pulled me on to his knee. Then he tried to kiss me.

"Ach, leave the girl alone," shouted the gross man. "No wonder she feels sick at the sight of that face. Who wouldn't? With me, of course, it is different," he crooned, winking at me and stroking his double chin. "Eh, my pretty?"

He seemed the most pleasantly disposed of the two, so unexpectedly jerking myself from the other man I walked over and sat on his knee. He was as flattered and delighted as the other was angry, and I realized I had made him my sworn champion. High words followed, but the lank one guessed he would come off worst in a fight, and so they made friends and split another bottle. It was only ten-thirty then, and I wondered how I was going to fare for the rest of the night. The gross man promptly answered that thought with a fierce snore. He was deep in alcoholic slumber. I hoped the brain of the younger man was too fuddled to appreciate the significance of that snore, and reasoned that in any case he would be less likely to try to molest me if I pretended to be asleep than if my eyes met his. But five minutes later the sound of a boot coming to the stone floor flags made me open my eyes. The lank man was standing regarding me. When my eyes opened he grinned all over his spotty face and meandered towards me. I tugged the sleeve of my champion but he would not wake up.

"Come, don't be a prude," muttered the lank soldier, stretching out his long arms to grip me. I fought wildly and got free, then dashed for the door. As I slipped through, a kitchen chair splintered against it, and filthy oaths slashed the cold night air. Then I was running hard under the friendly moon. A light showed in the Austrian telephone exchange hut, and I knew I could trust Austrians where I could not trust Germans. The two operators were surprised but kindly and nodded understandingly when I tried to explain. I spent the night on one of their bunks. Next day one of the German surgeons heard of my escape and took pity on me.

"See, Fräulein," he reassured me, "there shall be no more of this. I will arrange for you to sleep two houses from me, and my own batman shall conduct you to and from the hospital each day." I had the permit papers from Hooglede passed through the proper channels, and four days later I saw a little party of women enter the village at dusk and ran to greet my mother. We returned to live in the old house, and once more two guards came to look after us. Thus Christmas 1914 passed and the second year of the War began.

In January 1915 fortune temporarily favoured the Allies. Allied shells crashed steadily into Westroosebeke. Many casualties occurred in the streets, and to move from place to place was hazardous. The Kommandant summoned me.

"Fräulein, this place has become too dangerous. I have ordered that all the women shall go to Roulers. Do not worry, you will be escorted. You have done fine work here, and I shall recommend you to the authorities at Roulers."

And so next day we looked upon our native village for the last time before it disappeared under the maelstrom of war, and with our escort started sadly for Roulers along a highway thickly strewn with flax, and in places with old curtains and carpets, with bales of cloth and wool, through which the sticky mud oozed and squelched. Not content with confiscating all of last year's crop of flax, the Germans looted every house and shop of materials in Westroosebeke, to placate those overworked roads; but nothing could conquer that terrible mud!

CHAPTER II

Clad in rags and with all our worldly belongings piled high on one small handcart, we passed through the winding streets of the old country town of Roulers. What a difference six miles could make! We had come from an atmosphere of blood and desolation and smoking destruction to a welcoming spot whose gabled houses in their unharmed serenity held an air of refreshing peace. Civilians—busy about their own affairs—mingled with the swarms of soldiers in the streets, for apart from its large German garrison Roulers was a place of about 27,000 inhabitants. A bewildered little group of home-less women, we stood in the Grand Place and looked about us. A market was in progress and at first no one took much notice of us. We did not know where to go or what to do. My mother and I had learnt while we were at Westroosebeke that my father was somewhere in Roulers, but we had heard nothing from him since the night he was marched away under escort with the others. A well-dressed middle-aged woman approached us.

"You are refugees and you have nowhere to go to, isn't that so," she questioned us kindly. "I can take two of you as lodgers in my house, and I think I can arrange about accommodation for the rest with friends if you will come with me. . . ."

The house lay on the edge of the town overlooking the fields and an hour later my mother and I had sorted our possessions from the heap in the cart and, after depositing them in a large comfortable bedroom allotted to us by the middle-aged lady, were waiting in the warmth of the great open fire, which crackled on the kitchen hearth with its massive fire-dogs and iron spit, until the rest of the household gathered for the midday meal. This consisted of our hostess's husband, a prominent local grocer, her young sister who had fled from her convent school at the approach of the Germans, two German officers of the Army of Würtemberg billeted on the premises, an aged couple and a youngish woman and her small boy, refugees like ourselves. Our hostess promised to make inquiries in the town for my father, and thanks to her efforts he came to the house to see us two days later. For committing some minor breach of discipline he had been imprisoned for some considerable time, and since then he had worked for a farmer living on the outskirts of the town, with whom he lodged.

The Kommandant in Westroosebeke had handed me a letter written on my behalf by himself and also one written by the Army doctor whom I had worked under. I had instructions to take these to the senior Feldwebel at the Roulers hospital, and set out for the hospital the next morning, having made myself as presentable as possible in my old clothes, for until we could get in touch with my father we were without money.

Out along the Menin Road not far from Roulers stood the tall grey buildings of the College, set in spacious tree-shaded grounds, and from the battlements flew the Red Cross flag. A grey-headed, soldierly-looking officer was seated behind the desk in the well-furnished office into which an orderly ushered me near the pillared main entrance. He was the Oberartz, and after reading the letters I handed him, told me kindly that he would be more than grateful for any help which I should give to his hospital. I should be the only nurse there, although there were several Belgian women employed in cooking, washing and other domestic capacities.

The Oberartz asked me to lunch with him and the other surgeons, and every department of the hospital was explained to me. I was perhaps most struck with the civilian clinic, where civilians of the district suffering from every possible form of ailment were treated. The charges here were of the fairest, being based entirely on the means of the patient, and though rich people went away grumbling at the excessive fees, which were no more than they would have paid to a civil specialist, poor people paid little or nothing for the most skilled attention. To my certain knowledge there are many poor people of my district to-day who could never have hoped for a cure in all their lives but for treatment at the Roulers German Hospital. I agreed to start work at 7 a.m. on the Monday following, and was armed with a note to the Town-Kommandant from the Oberartz requesting that I should be given a night pass which would allow me out into the streets at any time of the night in case of an emergency call from the hospital; for curfew was enforced between 7 p.m. and 5 a.m., during which hours no unlicensed civilian might leave his house, and the streets were peopled only by soldiery.

Soon after my arrival at Roulers I was to find myself a participant in strange events of a nature which in my wildest dreams I had never pictured myself taking part, but before I plunge into the maelstrom I think it absolutely necessary, so that the reader can visualize Roulers under the Germans in 1915, to give a brief sketch of the life and conditions.

Roulers was under the control of a Town-Kommandant or military district magistrate who kept order throughout the town and environs with a body of military *gendarmerie*, a certain number of which acted as plain-clothes agents; and for their suspicious and overbearing behaviour these last were known as the "Berlin Vampires." Although under the military commander for the district for his orders, the Town-Kommandant, so far as we wretched civilians were concerned, was a demi-god. If he disapproved of something which the inhabitants had done he changed the curfew hour from 7 p.m. to 4 p.m. or even earlier, and perhaps fined the town a sum of money as well. He sentenced evil-doers (and not infrequently non-evil-doers whom his police brought before him) to terms of imprisonment. He was very vigilant in the nosing out of spies and food hoarders, and during the daylight hour all houses had to be left open so that his agents might walk in to take a look round whenever they pleased. Troops and their officers were billeted in every house of any size, and there was an aerodrome on the outskirts, so that Roulers was subject to occasional air raids. It had at one time been shelled heavily as certain roofless and pock-marked buildings testified; but in 1915 only a stray shell or two crumpled down in the vicinity, doing little damage.

Many of the refugee women who had found refuge in the town were utterly destitute and a large number of these, with girls recruited locally, were well paid by the Germans to manufacture sandbags and other necessities. These sandbags were made of all kinds of odd material such as silk, velvet, and cretonne, anything which could be procured from the local merchants, in fact. At the time of our arrival three girl sandbag-makers were undergoing a prison sentence for having succumbed to temptation. Having been allotted some peculiarly pretty lengths of patterned silk for their bags, they contrived to smuggle this off the premises to make dresses for themselves, but were unfortunately asked to disclose what they carried in their parcels by an inquisitive "Berlin Vampire." These "martyrs," however, set a fashion in crime, for clothes were already expensive to procure and were to become far more so.

Seventy-five per cent of every sort of product was claimed by the German Levying Commission; the civilians scrambled for the remaining 25 per cent, and had it not been for the American Relief Commission the suffering would have been terrible. Supplies came to Antwerp direct from the U.S.A., and all vessels bearing an American flag which were marked in a certain way were allowed through the submarine blockade. The organizer of the Relief Commission was Mr. Hoover, the late U.S. President. At Antwerp the ships were unloaded under a mixed commission of Americans and Belgians, and the food was distributed to towns and departments in accordance with the indents sent in by local civil committees, reaching their destination either by rail or road, whichever the German authorities could spare for transport purposes at the moment. Seals were placed on the bales of goods and strict orders were issued that nothing should be touched. As a rule it never was; but there were occasions when some German regiment *en route* looted the sealed vehicles on the quiet.

Bacon, putrid stuff nicknamed "Wilson" by the disgusted civilians, rice, meal, small quantities of sugar and a kind of broken maize called *cerealing* by the Relief Commission and "Hoover" by those who had to eat it, were the only foodstuffs the Commission supplied, and although we grumbled at the quality we were at heart exceedingly grateful to get the food. Upon arrival in Roulers the consignment was sorted and removed to an empty shop in the town, and here we repaired with our ration cards to buy as much as they would allow us at extremely reasonable prices. There were times when the quantities for sale were tragically short.

As for the general conduct of the Germans in the place, they were the conquerors and we must not forget the fact, but to those Belgians with whom they were brought in close contact they were guardedly friendly. There were, of course, incidents such as occur in any garrison town in war-time, but the troops were under strict discipline. As for us, there was among the civilians an atmosphere of continual silent antagonism; antagonism not so much against individuals but against the harsh German yoke and the minions who maintained it.

One morning, a fortnight after our arrival, I had returned after night-duty to our lodging. It was about seven o'clock in the morning and nobody was about but my mother, to whom I was talking in the kitchen. There was no knock, but suddenly the back-door creaked and the handle began to turn, so that our eyes became riveted upon it. In the entrance stood Lucelle Deldonck, her grey hair hanging in wisps, her face ghastly with fatigue. She put a finger to her lips for silence, while my mother helped her to a chair.

"No one must know that I have been here," she told us in a low voice. "I have had much difficulty in finding you, and had I not seen through the kitchen window that you were alone, I should not have come in now."

By that time we had finally given her up as lost, and we listened amazed to the inexplicable way in which she was talking, the while she gulped some brandy which I had handed her.

"But where have you come from, Lucelle?"

"From over the frontier and I have news for you. Your three sons are all safe, with the Army at the Yser. Here are three letters. My own family are also safe, thank God—but to let you know this is not the reason which brings me to Roulers—listen," she chuckled; "I am a middle-aged woman and I thought last year that I was in a good way to spend the rest of my days in peace and quietness. But I tell you, I have just tramped forty or so miles from Holland, and I have a further ten miles to go. Should the Germans know I was here it would mean——"

She stopped dead as though a hand had been clapped over her mouth. Then she rose wearily.

"Well, I must be going," she finished, "I am glad to have seen you both again. Remember, no one must know that I have been in this town." At the door she paused as if a thought had struck her and looked hard at me. "Martha," she said slowly, "you are young and strong. Would you like to serve your country?"

I knew what she must mean, a spy, and for a moment I was filled with horror. I knew that spies existed in Belgium and that they were serving their country, yet somehow I had regarded them as things inhuman and far removed from my own sphere.

"If my daughter wishes to serve I give her willingly and proudly, just as I have given my sons," exclaimed my mother, placing her hands gently on my shoulders.

"You realize that in this occupation your life will be at stake every day of your life, Martha. What do you say?"

Things were beginning to appear to me in a new light.

"I am waiting for my instructions, Lucelle," was my reply.

"Brave girl, Martha. At present I shall give you no instructions. I am a member of the British Secret Intelligence Commission. I can tell you nothing until I have communicated with them, for it is from them ultimately that you will get your orders. In a few days' time expect to receive a summons from me, and in whatever manner this comes to you show no surprise. For a few days there are matters which will keep me not far from Roulers. And now, good-bye," she smiled; "I am going away across the open fields like most of we travellers do who have no pass from the Germans."

Then she had slipped away, leaving my mother and me staring into each other's eyes, but neither of us spoke a word of what had passed.

There was an old vegetable woman, nicknamed by the German soldiers "Canteen Ma" and a great favourite among them, who used to come in from the country several times a week with fruit and vegetables in a four-wheeled car, calling at the houses of her various clients for orders. Her pass to move freely about the countryside existed owing to the fact that she had a contract to supply the German Canteen with fruit. She was nearly seventy years old with white elfin locks and the cheeks of a schoolboy. It was three days after Lucelle's visit and I was just leaving for the hospital in the early morning when I saw her after her usual manner coming down the street leading her old nag and singing and whistling to herself some old-time chanson of the people.

"Good day, Mademoiselle," she hailed in her high cracked voice, approaching with a basket on her arm. "It's cold, but a beautiful morning to be out early. What about some nice beans, Mademoiselle—cheap to-day."

I was about to call the servant girl when Canteen Ma stooped to put her basket down on the step and at the same moment slipped something small into my hand.

"Take a look at that in the seclusion of your bedroom," she whispered.

The servant came at my call and I hurried tremblingly upstairs to my room and shut the door. It was a small piece of intricately folded paper.

"Come to the second farm on the right-hand side of the road to Zwevezeele. Ask for Lisette, who is expecting to see you at nine o'clock to-night."

read the anonymous contents. The idea crossed my mind that it might be a trap of the "Berlin Vampires," but I determined to risk that. If it was from Lucelle I must see her at all costs.

I determined to take no risks with "Vampires" on the roads that evening and gave myself a full hour to reach my destination, making a wide detour across the fields. I must admit my heart was in my mouth. My only excuse, in case I was questioned, for being in the fields at that hour would be that I had been asked to visit a sick woman in my capacity as trained nurse. The ground was hard with frost which made the going easy. Here and there soldiers carrying lights were moving along the footpaths. After what seemed an eternity I came out on the road some distance beyond the farm, and that short space of time during which I was retracing my steps was the most nerve-racking of the evening.

At the back-door I knocked like a conspirator, realizing that for better or for worse I had finally taken my life into my hands. The door creaked slightly.

"What do you want?" asked a muffled voice.

"I have come to see Lisette."

A grunt, shuffling of feet on the stone slabs and the door opened wide on to a dark passage. A figure was standing well back against the wall. Unexpectedly a hand grasped and hurried me up an unlit flight of stairs somewhere at the back of the house. I was pushed into a room with heavily curtained windows, illuminated only by the dancing flames of the fire.

"Pierre," said Lucelle, who was standing with her back to the hearth. "Give me good warning if you hear anything suspicious." Then we were alone. "Child, I rejoice to see you."

Lucelle motioned me to a chair beside the fire and seated herself opposite.

"Martha," Lucelle started, "from this day forward at your own wish you have become a spy in the service of the enemies of the conquerors who now rule your country. From time to time you will receive certain orders or instructions and you will comply with these to the best of your ability. In your position as nurse at the Roulers Hospital, where you will be constantly in contact with enemy soldiers of all ranks, you will have exceptional opportunities of learning of troop movements, locations of military formations, artillery concentrations and positions, the forming of supply dumps and of all the numerous military activities which take place daily in a garrison town near the line. Apart, therefore, from the execution of special orders it will be your duty to report all military information, even if it may seem to you of the smallest importance. Remember, it is not for you to judge the significance of what you may learn and what you see around you. There are military experts over the frontier who will understand how to sift the information."

"But how am I to transmit my reports?" I put in.

"Have a little patience, Martha, and you will learn everything. Let us start at the beginning. To the British

Intelligence you are known as 'Laura.' You will send all your messages in code signed that name. The code you will use is ingenious, yet easily mastered or deciphered by anyone possessing the key. The first of your tasks will be to learn the formula of this code by heart so thoroughly that you will never, never make a mistake. The moment you have done this you will destroy the formula; you can understand that for your own safety the sooner you have burnt such a damning piece of evidence the better."

I took the folded paper which Lucelle handed me without any comment, and pushed it in the top of my stocking. Lucelle chuckled quietly.

"That is not a very clever or original place to hide such a dangerous piece of paper, Martha. If anyone were to search you that is the first place they would look. Put it in your hair. And now to continue. You will receive your instructions through the old vegetable woman, known among the Germans as Canteen Ma. When you have a message to send, after coding it you go down the Rue de la Place until you reach the Grand Place. Next on the right here you will see an alleyway. Enter this, tap three times, pause, then tap twice again on the fifth window on the left-hand side, then wait. One of our agents there, known as 'No. 63,' will take your message, which will be transmitted at once to the British Intelligence Section over the frontier by a number of volunteer runners in relays, for it is unwise for a message ever to remain in the same hands for long——"

When I had assured her that I understood perfectly what I was to do, Lucelle went on once again. She told me to destroy every message I received directly I had read it, and advised me that when I had written a message for transmission I should take it to No. 63 immediately and not conceal it in the house until some seemingly more auspicious time. Then she told me of the "safety-pin men," who were apparently a very active branch of the anti-German espionage system. These men sometimes carried out the most desperate and astonishing enterprises. I should know a "safety-pin man" by the two white-metal safety-pins which he carried beneath the lapel of his coat. In a few days, she said, a strange man would call at our house and ask for me. If he showed me two safety-pins in his lapel, I was to do my best to persuade my hostess either to give him lodging in the house or to find him lodgings with her friends near by. This man was in Roulers "on a special mission" and would perhaps only remain a short time. During that time I was to take any message he might wish to transmit and give it to No. 63.

Lucelle rose.

"Unfortunately, Martha, I have reason to believe that the 'Vampires' know that I am in this district. I shall leave to-night as soon as you have gone, and I hope to have crossed the frontier at an early hour to-morrow. A little, general advice, Martha—a spy needs above all else to keep her wits about her every moment of her life, asleep or awake—eyes, ears, brains and intelligence are the tools of the good spy. If you are caught it will in all probability be your own fault. Remember, in everything you say, in everything you do, you must give the impression that the very last thing in the world you would think of being is a spy—there may be other spies working around you, but do not bother yourself with their activities unless it is necessary in the course of your work; the less you know of your fellow-spies the less the 'Vampires' are likely to wring out of you if they catch you. Good-bye, Martha, and God be with you."

The house seemed deserted as I groped my way downstairs, but a hand caught my wrist as I reached the foot, led me through the darkness, and I was let out through the same door by which I had entered.

Two days later my mother told me when I came in from the hospital that a man had called earlier in the day, asking for me. I had warned her that such a man might come, and that if I happened to be out at the time, she was to ask him to return when I should be at home. He came to the door again soon afterwards. He was a big, handsome, moustached fellow of middle age in the clothes of a labouring man.

"Good day, Mademoiselle, is there any chance of finding lodging here. I'm one of the unfortunate ones who lost pretty well everything in the invasion. They tell me the work up here is well paid for, so I'm going to try my luck——"

"Step inside for a moment," I invited, "and I will ask the owner of this house what she can do for you." Directly he was within the shelter of the doorway he shot a quick glance about him to see that he was unobserved, then hastily lifted his lapel and for a fleeting instant I saw two metal safety-pins. He was a cheerful type of man for whom my hostess seemed to take an instant fancy. She offered him a bed in the attic, the only space in the house still un-occupied, and the stranger accepted gratefully. Within an hour this mysterious stranger was on the friendliest terms with every one in the house, including the two German officers. He spoke fluent German, good French and fair Flemish, and was evidently a man of good class.

Thanks to him, the evening meal that night and for many nights to come was a hilarious affair. He had apparently been Jack-of-all-trades in his time, from seaman to engineer in the Argentine, and poured forth an amazing flow of anecdotes of a distinctly Rabelaisian character. The two Germans were so pleased with him that they used to treat him in their room or in one of the cafés to orgies of wine and cigars. They must have somehow procured him a special pass, for there were nights when I let the three of them in, stumbling and noisily intoxicated, hours after the official curfew. I do not think the stranger was ever really drunk on those occasions, for although be always roared as loudly as the others, I well remember the night that he deliberately turned and winked at me while the Germans were groping their way up the stairs ahead of him.

Also, certain sounds which I heard in the house at times after midnight made me think that the stranger was in the habit of making excursions on his own account. I was out at the hospital for the greater part of the day, and a whole week passed without the stranger having addressed a single word to me when we were alone together, nor did he appear to seek any such opportunity. Then one evening I came upon him standing by himself in the kitchen, puffing spasmodically at his pipe and gazing thoughtfully into the flames.

"Good evening, Mademoiselle," he nodded, "it's a cold night outside, eh?" Then he threw that quick searching glance round him which I had seen before. "I think perhaps you will know what to do with this," he murmured, drawing a cylinder of white paper from his cigarette-case and slipping it into my hand.

"It will go to-night," I assured him, with something of a thrill, for this was my first job. I should meet No. 63. I wondered whether it was a he or a she, and what that personage was like. I looked at the stranger and he was staring into the fire again.

"What are you doing here?" I ventured.

"Secret Service," came the gruff reply, "that is good enough—" He looked up sharply. "After all it strikes me that there is something that I should tell you, Mademoiselle. —As a rule we safety-pin men prefer to work alone, but it is possible that at some time in the future you may be approached by a safety-pin man who needs your assistance.—When such a man shows you his pins note the manner in which they are placed under his lapel. It is a new order, this, unless the pins run diagonally across the lapel he will not be a safety-pin man at all, and you will pretend you are puzzled at the pins. He will be a 'Vampire'; for the Germans know of the safety-pin men, and I know that there *are* certain agents here who are masquerading as such. In fact, to locate and identify these false safety-pin men constitutes one of the main reasons for my being here—When I come face to face with one of these men I do not propose to let him off lightly," he growled between set teeth.—It was at this point that he stopped talking, for we heard the voices of the two German officers in the front hall.

The church clock chimed ten o'clock just after I had stealthily let myself out of the back door to embark on my first official mission. In case I was stopped my pass would help me, but that did not protect me from any inquisitive agent who wished to search me. The little scroll of paper was in my hair. The streets were dark, for the lamps were shaded, but I passed many soldiers on the way to their billets. Near the corner of the alleyway a German Gefreiter was chatting with a gendarme. They eyed me with suspicion and I felt cold sweat trickle down my forehead as I walked straight on past my destination. Was the gendarme going to stop me? Out of the corner of my eye I saw the men make a move, and my heart seemed to stop beating. But they only walked off talking together and the black mouth of the alley was empty. Like a flash I was up the alley and had stopped at the fifth window on the left-hand side. I executed the sequence of taps that

Lucelle had taught me, making sure that there were no eyes at all in those other windows so carefully covered with brown paper. I was trembling so much that my knees shook. What if a patrolling gendarme stopped at the entrance to the alleyway? Suppose he came down into the darkness and found me quaking there, with no real excuse for being abroad?

Suddenly and without a sound the window slid upward a few inches. A hand—white against the darkness—came out. Into it I thrust my precious slip of paper. Then the hand retreated, the window was closed and all was as before. The affair was over bar the grisly business of getting safely out of the alley. I was reaching the mouth when I saw a German methodically tramping his beat. He passed. Then, with my heart thudding in my throat, I took the plunge. Presently I was hurrying along the wide streets but keeping well in the shadows. Out here I might excuse myself by saying that I was returning from the hospital. By taking a short cut I was soon at the house. I *had succeeded*. The thought set my pulses racing. I was serving my country and I had risked my life. It all seemed so absurdly easy then but that was only the beginning.

CHAPTER III

During the succeeding days I kept my eyes very wide open and my ears always on the alert. It was the rickety old steam-trams of Roulers, which the German troops had nicknamed "Ca-ne-fait-rien" because they were continuously breaking down, which gave me my first idea. I used to pass them, puffing and rattling and leaving great clouds of dirty black smoke behind them, as they regularly carried resigned-looking soldiers or loads of shells or rifle ammunition up to the German second line. These had been fetched from the railway station, and I noticed that on one day of every week, which always varied from its predecessor, the trams would be exceedingly active in taking ammunition up to the front for about twelve hours. This fact set me to keeping an eye on the trains halting at Roulers, and I soon knew for certainty that the weekly activity of trams indicated the weekly arrival of an Ordnance train, and that this would take about twelve hours to unload.

If only I could discover the day and time of arrival of a weekly Ordnance train, I might inform the British air-craft through the medium of No. 63, and the station could be bombed. The only way to get the necessary information was to make friends with one of the German military railway transport officials, in hopes he would give something away unwittingly. I had ample excuse for going to the station, as I was often detailed to escort German wounded there in the ambulance who were being sent to hospitals farther back.

One sunny afternoon I stood on the platform watching a train with some of my wounded gliding into the distance. It was a slack time and they did not need me at the hospital for two hours. I had told the ambulance driver I would walk back slowly as it was a lovely day. The thought had just occurred to me that unless I could find some specific excuse to remain in the station it would be advisable to leave, when a voice behind me chirped:

"Liebe Fräulein, I am charmed that you should with your lovely presence so often this station grace."

A little round officer with a pleasant, florid face saluted me with a smirk. I had caught his rather bulbous blue eyes wandering in my direction during my station visits for several weeks past. From the way he strutted about the station, occasionally glancing down to admire the glassy polish which he maintained on his field-boots, I guessed that his Staff post was still a novelty, the dignity of which he enjoyed immensely.

"I was enjoying the beautiful weather," I smiled. "For once we are not busy at the hospital, and I have a few hours to myself. You, of course, Herr Hauptmann, are more than fully occupied with your heavy duties."

"No, Fräulein," he preened himself, "for the first time in days I too am free."

Looking highly pleased with the way matters were progressing between us, he drew out his cigarette-case.

"You will smoke, Fräulein?"

"Not in the open, thank you, Herr Hauptmann."

"Ah, that is simple, come along to my office, Fräulein—do allow me to give you tea there."

Three minutes later we were sitting in his inner office enjoying cigarettes, while outside convict-shaven orderlies were answering the persistent telephone and hammering typewriters. For about a quarter of an hour our conversation was trivial. Whenever I looked away from him I knew that he was watching me. I realized that my determination to find what I wanted had driven out all nervousness, and I was deliberately enjoying myself.

"In Belgium I am lost," he mourned, dismally following the curling spiral of cigarette smoke. "I am a widower, but in Hanover I have my two young daughters, and they mean much to me."

"So, he is a widower," I thought complacently to myself, and seating myself on the office table beside his chair, gazed down upon him with eyes of sympathy.

"Yes, war is terrible," I said. "The whole thing is so futile and so sad."

As though by accident, I felt his podgy little hand close over mine. I did not move. I felt that he was becoming "malleable." The door opened and an orderly clicked to attention.

"You are wanted urgently on the telephone, sir."

He re-entered a few minutes later.

"Well, Fräulein, it is work for me as usual, and at once."

I rose to leave, and as I hoped it had the desired effect.

"Fräulein," he told me, "I hope that I shall see you again. Perhaps there is some time when we are both free when we could go out together."

"There is nothing I should like better," I nodded meltingly. "It is Monday to-day, for what parts of this week are you free?"

He dived eagerly into a notebook, and I had no difficulty in looking over his shoulder. Under WEDNESDAY I read:

"Ordnance train—arrive 3 a.m.—depart 3 p.m. Shells heavy calibre to local dumps as ordered later. Shells light calibre and small-arms ammunition to continue up line by tram."

The little man looked up smiling happily.

"Friday afternoon and evening, Liebe Fräulein, would suit me well. I could get a special pass, and we might run over to Ghent and spend a really nice evening! What do you say?"

He caught my hands and smirked up at me. Somehow it made me think of a puppy with its tongue hanging out. I pretended to think a moment.

"Yes," I said slowly; "we will spend Friday afternoon and evening together—and we will have a really good time!" I loosed my hands, opened the door, and with a soft glance over my shoulder bid "Good-bye" to the bowing form of my comic little cavalier.

If my plans came off there would be no Friday evening for him!—And I hoped there would not be much of his station left either. It was not until the outer office was left behind me that I fully realized the grim task which I had accepted. For a moment ghastly terror shook me in every limb. Was I—quiet, harmless Martha Cnockaert—really about to do this terrible thing? The terror passed and black gloom surrounded me, but piercing this there suddenly flashed a vision of my country, scarred and bleeding beneath the German fieldboot.

I thought of the thousands of my countrymen who had died in battle, or lingered on to gasp out their lives in fearful anguish. I thought of the aged priest digging his own grave, of a maddened woman who hurled herself from a window when the soldiers had finished with her, of those streams of innocent flotsam of the grey tidal wave. Quickening my footsteps I reached home fierce and breathless, wrote the necessary information regarding the hours the Ordnance train would lie in the station, and concealed the scrap of paper in my hair. When I got away from the hospital that evening I would take it round to No. 63.—If only that mysterious he or she could get the news to the British Flying Corps in time—well, Roulers was a smallish station, and if the ammunition train blew up there would certainly not be much of it left!

All that afternoon and evening at the hospital I could not concentrate upon the work in hand. Twice the surgeon found fault with me irritably, and my nerves had become so on edge that involuntarily I found myself weeping. I had had to stay later than usual because it was necessary for me to attend at an emergency operation. The Oberartz evidently thought I was overwrought.

"Take this sedative, Fräulein," he urged gently; "we can finish without you to-night. Go home right away and get a long night's rest, and let me know how you feel to-morrow."

He was a dear, that grey-headed chief-surgeon, and unselfish, too. But, on that night, he could not have thought of a better way of helping me. It was dark, and the streets were deserted. The darkened street-lamps threw pools of light on to the pavement, outside whose radiance I twice heard patrols tramp by me. Either they recognized me or were intent on other things, for I went unchallenged. Away by Ypres the guns were growling and thudding, and the western horizon flickered with the rising lights of Véry shells. I paused at the mouth of the alleyway, but all was silence. Then I slipped towards the fifth window and tapped.

As before it slid upwards noiselessly, and the white hand appeared and vanished with my note. With a sense of wonderful relief I returned home. The affair now was out of my hands, at any rate, I could do nothing either to promote or avert disaster. I could only wait. . . .

~

He was standing under the light of the lantern in the passage as I opened the front door, a tall military policeman.

"Fräulein Cnockaert?" he asked gruffly.

My head leapt to my mouth and ice-cold beads of perspiration burst out on my brow. Unable to speak, I nodded, and swallowed hard to still my rising agitation.

"Please come with me," the man went on. "The officers have some questions they wish to put to you."

The pounding of my heart seemed to fill the whole passage with sound as I dumbly followed the soldier into the kitchen like one going to execution. Two officers of military police whom I knew well by sight sat at the table. They rose as I entered and bowed punctiliously.

"Will not the Fräulein sit?" suggested he whom I took to be the senior of the two, a stocky man with red hair.

In a dream I sat down in the chair which he pushed towards me. I was dazed at this sudden turn of events. What had the German police discovered? Was my career as a secret agent of Belgium to be ended after this first coup? I heard my interrogator's voice as something far away.

"Fräulein Cnockaert," he said. "What has become of the woman, Lucelle Deldonck? She is your friend—eh? She was seen in Roulers very recently."

There was a pause. A dead weight lay over my heart and my nails dug into the perspiration-soaked palms of my hands. The officer leaned towards me.

"Where is Lucelle Deldonck, now?" he pronounced slowly, watching me closely.

I shrugged my shoulders feebly, numbed into silence. Then they did know of my double rôle!

"Do not be afraid, Fräulein," soothed the officer; "just tell us all that you know."

Still I did not answer. The eyes of the three men bored steadily into me, and everything was whirling. I kept telling myself I must say something. Every moment I delayed must tend to make the men more suspicious. I took a grip on myself.

"Lucelle Deldonck disappeared when your soldiers raided the cellar in Westroosebeke where we and many other harmless people had taken refuge. For all I know they may have I killed her. Most of them were drunk, and they were certainly free enough with their weapons."

The red-haired man was silent for a while, and clearly in two minds as to whether I was speaking the truth or not. Impatiently he thrust a cigarette into his lips, twisted a paper taper, and turned his back, thrusting it into the fire. Suddenly he whirled round.

"Fräulein," he rapped, through a cloud of blue smoke. "Are you sure you have not seen Lucelle Deldonck? Think carefully now. Has she not been in this room only lately?——"

"She has not. I have not seen her since we left Westroosebeke, I tell you."

I looked him square in the eyes.

Apparently he was satisfied. Signing to his companions to go and stamping his newly lighted cigarette out on the floor, he left the kitchen with a "Very well, Fräulein Cnockaert. Perhaps we have worried you unnecessarily considering the excellent work which I am told you are doing for our wounded in the hospital. After all, it is Lucelle Deldonck and not you that we want. But be very careful. I have certain information, perhaps not reliable, that she has been in Roulers. I should be sorry to have to report you to the Town-Kommandant as a suspicious character."

Quickly I ran to the window and watched the three men disappear round the corner at the bottom of the street. They had really gone; I breathed a sigh of relief. I prayed that there would be no more of these nerve-racking examinations, and I prayed, too, that Lucelle would evade capture, for it was plain that the Germans had marked her for a spy.

Within five minutes I was alone in my own room, the police forgotten, wondering, hoping, fearing, what would be the result of that information I had passed to No. 63. Would the English bomb the whole town? If so we might ourselves be killed. For the succeeding days I lived on my nerves, on the very edge of expectancy. I could neither eat nor sleep, and the kind Oberartz was perturbed and gave me tonics. I swallowed these, feeling I was betraying the hand that helped me. Yet what was I to do? I was pledged to Lucelle, to the British just over there in the darkness who were fighting and dying hour by hour. I must harden my mind. On Wednesday night I tossed feverishly on my bed through an eternity of darkness. At last, shaking, I lit the lamp. It was a quarter past three. The Ordnance train had arrived in the station!

I extinguished the light, and must have fallen into a doze.

"Martha, Martha, to the cellar!" My mother leaned over the bed shaking me.

Outside the night was hideous with the crashing barrage of anti-aircraft guns, the shrieking of syrens, the shouting of men and the clatter of hurrying feet. Once in a lull of the firing I heard the sinister growl of engines, a purr which spelt flaming death to the watchers below. I leaped out of bed, threw a cloak over my nightdress and tore downstairs, and crouched fascinated in the open doorway. Silver knives of the searchlights were slicing the sky, quartering this way and that. Transcending all sounds came that whistling moan of a descending bomb, a distant flash over the roof-tops, an earth-shaking thud. The bomb had missed its mark. Machine-guns spat savagely from posts on the roofs, yellow and scarlet stars blossomed against the clouds, shrapnel seeking the raiders; but of these I could make out nothing. I felt a thrilling sense of exaltation. The British had had my message. It was I who was responsible for the hellish scene which was now being enacted. Pray God they hit that long train in the siding, loaded with death and torture for themselves and their Allies.

My heart stopped a beat. One lone white speck was hovering in those relentless beams of light in the sky. One aeroplane? I could not believe my eyes! But after watching for a few minutes I was certain that was all. It seemed madness to send just a single machine in the face of that raging, tearing hurricane of German shot. I found myself shivering with apprehension out upon the cold wind-swept pavement. The idiots—the fools—why had they taken a thousand to one chance instead of making certain!

Suddenly that white speck plunged earth-ward. It had been hit. It was hurtling to destruction on our very heads. The chorus of guns swelled to a deep diapason, men were cheering all round me. Then, miraculously, the zooming plane flattened out with a roar just as it seemed about to crumple against the housetops. Above the shriek of the shells sounded a deep thud, but still that Ordnance train waited unscathed.

A vast sheet of flame silhouetted the whole town in its glare. The atmosphere quivered, and a thundering detonation hurled me against the wall. The air seemed raining stones, slates avalanched from the roofs upon the pavements, all Roulers was shaking, and there was the tinkling of falling glass from a thousand windows. Men in the street screamed and threw themselves face downward. Then followed explosion after explosion, and the staccato pop of myriads of detonating rifle bullets. That last bomb had struck the Ordnance train fair and square. Two score roofs in Roulers were torn off in that maelstrom of destruction!

From where I lay in the doorway I watched breathlessly as the raiding plane twisted and turned as it climbed back to the clouds. From its tail streamed a tongue of red fire, broadening, brightening. It wavered, then spiralled headlong downwards, smashing into the ground at 100 m.p.h. The play was over. In the dawn two British airmen were found, still breathing, but smashed and unconscious. They had done their job, and for them nothing more mattered, save a short interval of agony before the final peace. The machine was a twisted, blackened mass of steel, wood and canvas, a poor wreck of the monarch that such a short time before had ridden the clouds.

I had succeeded in my small part. Then I remembered those lads, burned and broken, who but for me and my warnings would not have crashed to the earth with their machine in a holocaust of flame. As I crept upstairs I was thinking of the smoking ruins of the station, and of the fate of my little German officer friend of the Railway Transport. The groans of the mangled Germans whom I knew must lie thick about the station seemed ringing in my ears. I threw myself on my bed, turned my face to the wall and wept as though my heart was breaking——

~

For three days after that the nights were a torture, interspersed with bouts of feverish nightmare in which I wandered along an endless street of smoking ruins where the way was strewn with mangled corpses whose glassy eyeballs watched me accusingly. At the hospital I jumped at every unfamiliar sound, my hands trembled and I dragged myself about as if in a dream. The Oberartz gave me more tonics and several times urged me to go home, where he offered personally to come and examine me. But I knew that to spend my days lying in bed would give me leisure to think those terrible thoughts, and I insisted upon continuing, for in time I knew I would conquer my weakness and become resolute once again.

It was upon the afternoon of the fourth day that I overheard a conversation in the passage-way outside the half-open door of my ward. It was the Oberartz speaking:

"This is the Devil . . . Lichienstein of No. 3 Advanced Dressing Station mortally wounded. He was a splendid fellow, I am truly sorry—but it is all very well for the Brigade to order me to supply a temporary relief. Aufrecht and Nagle went to No. 8 Hospital this morning and their reliefs have not arrived, so that we are short-handed. Sudermann is down with pneumonia, and is out of the question. There remains only myself. How can I leave the hospital without one single doctor?——"

"Have you not an Unter-offizier who could deputize for a doctor temporarily, Herr Oberartz?" suggested an unfamiliar voice.

"It seems the only way. But you understand, Herr Hauptmann, an Unter-offizier although an excellent dresser has in no sense the training and understanding of a doctor. Nor can he under any circumstances perform an urgent operation."

The idea seemed to strike me like a flash of lightning. Almost before I knew it I found myself out in the passage facing the Oberartz and a Staff-Hauptmann.

"Herr Oberartz," I said, "I will work at the advanced dressing-station till the relief comes. I had completed much of my training as a medical student when war broke out. I am far better qualified than is any non-commissioned officer."

"Impossible, Fräulein," sentenced the Oberartz, "you are a woman!" and the Staff Hauptmann gaped.

"This is a case of emergency," I put in. "I have volunteered of my own free will to go. My sex has nothing to do with it."

"Up at the advanced dressing-stations it is no joke, Fräulein. You realize you will be in constant danger?"

"I shall be ready whenever you wish me to go." The Oberartz bowed. "I thank you, Fräulein," he said quietly.

"I shall, of course, report your conduct at Brigade, Fräulein," offered the Hauptmann, shaking my hand. Then he saluted and hurried away to his other duties.

An hour later I sat beside the driver of a battered ambulance, muffled in a German military great-coat, while rain lashed against the cracked windscreen, and we ploughed and rocked through the soupy mire of an execrable country road toward the ever-loudening rumble of gun-fire. An express train seemed to shriek overhead, followed by a dull roar behind us.

"First shell to welcome us," laughed the driver. "The Allies seem to be taking it easy this afternoon. I hope for your sake they continue to do so, Fräulein."

A few minutes later we splashed to a standstill in a little shattered wood. "Advanced Dressing-Station No. 3," read a dirty white signboard over the wide sandbagged mouth of a dugout in the bank of the roadside. I remember well noticing two solitary snowdrops sprouting side by side in that desolate bank as I stepped from the footboard into the mud. "Good luck, Fräulein," shouted the driver, through the curtain of driving rain, and then he threw in his clutch and rattled away. A medical Feldwebel met me in the entrance with a salute. "The Herr Oberartz of the hospital 'phoned saying you would arrive, Fräulein. This is a hell of a place, I'm afraid; but we do the best we can. Sometimes we work day and night without a break, but temporarily there is a lull up in front." We descended the slimy stairs.

A sickening stench of blood, disinfectant and stale perspiration greeted my nostrils. Two central hurricane lamps hanging low over a rough kitchen table, wet with ominous stains, lit a large dugout with boarded walls. Four corpses covered with overcoats lay stretched in a far corner, and opposite squatted three medical orderlies laughing and smoking. A Gefreiter, who from the state of his clothing might have been a slaughter-house assistant, stopped whistling and, rising from the case of dressings he was checking, touched his cap. A very muddy British soldier, whose naked chest was swathed in bandages, and an equally filthy German, with a great white turban on his head, watched me from their place against the blood-splashed wall. The Feldwebel pulled forward a box.

"Sit down, Fräulein," he invited. "A lot of noise has started up overhead. I think perhaps we shall have some work to do before long. I daresay you are hungry?" He thrust a lump of bread with a large slice of tinned meat into my hand, and called to an orderly to get me a mug of coffee from a small stove in the corner.

"I'm not hungry, thanks," I remonstrated.

"Better eat now—must have strength—and maybe you'll not feel much like eating when the cases begin to arrive."

Voices and splashing footsteps sounded outside.—"Here they come," ejaculated the Feldwebel, cheerfully wiping his long moustache. "Now, get moving, lads." The orderlies rose, stamped out their cigarettes, and rolling their sleeves, went to the foot of the steps.

All through the night the Allies shelled heavily and the wounded continued to dribble in, tattered wretches smeared with mud and blood using their rifles as crutches, men staggering arm-in-arm, singing as if drunk, groping men with bandaged eyes, and those screaming wrecks of humanity lowered down the steps by the slithering, swearing, perspiring stretcher-bearers. Now and then as a man lay on the table to be dressed or probed or amputated, a shell pounded the ground above, and earth and stones rained down into the open wounds of the writhing patients. A man yelled for morphia, and other sufferers took up the cry till it became a continual wail.

"There is no morphia here, Fräulein," the Feldwebel answered my inquiry. "Why, if we gave all the men morphia who asked for it, we should need great tanks of it!" He took a hypodermic syringe and filled it from a bottle of liquid labelled "Morphia."—"This answers as well in most cases," he said in passing, and proceeded to make injections into the sufferers, prominently displaying the labelled bottle the while. At once the moans quietened and many lay still.

"What is in the bottle?" I asked him.

"Water," he told me in an undertone.

I thought about little except the task in hand, and hardly noticed how the time flew. About dawn the Feldwebel brought me enough spirits in a mug to make me unconscious under normal circumstances. As it was I hardly noticed the effect. I was covered with dirt from the ceiling, and my forehead was bleeding where a stone splinter had struck me. Two memories alone stand out clearly during those suffocating hours in the dressing-station. One was the conduct of the British soldier with the bandaged chest who had been propped up against the dugout wall when I entered, and the other was the entrance of the "Scot."

The Englishman was a cheery little rubicund man with his cap at the back of his head. He whiled away the time droning on a tinny mouth-organ, and smoking cigarettes, of which he seemed to have an endless supply in his pockets. In the hustle to evacuate the German wounded he was taken little notice of, and when men who had been attended to were from time to time helped up the steps to the waiting ambulance he shouted hoarsely, "'Ere, you're forgettin' me, aren't yer?" A complaint which nobody understood except myself, and he had roared it out five times before I could grasp his meaning. After each of his unsuccessful vocal efforts, the little man smiled to himself philosophically, and just to show that in spite of it all he bore no ill-will to the Huns, invariably offered the men laid beside him a cigarette and shot remarks at them in "pidgin" English, even if they were on the point of death.

A German lieutenant of slim and haughty appearance was waiting to have his badly shattered hand dressed, and was standing near the Englishman. The lieutenant flicked his gold cigarette-case from his tunic pocket and found it empty. The British "Tommy" saw this. He tapped the lieutenant's well-fitting field-boot with a grimy hand.

"'Ere," he invited thrusting up a paper packet, "take one of these, sir."

The lieutenant's eyes flashed.

"What—you swine," he hissed. "Don't speak to me like that," and he kicked "Tommy" savagely on the leg.

"Tommy" withdrew his despised packet quietly.

"Crikey," he said, "you're a real gentleman, you are.—Well, yer don't object if Fritz here and I has a smoke, do yer?"

The young officer obviously understood and was seething with rage, when fortunately the arrival of the "Scot," who had slipped from half-way down the soggy dugout steps with an oath of pain, and much clatter, brought all eyes in his direction. It was my first sight of a Highland soldier, and I thought at first he had lost his trousers. A long, cadaverous man with very dirty, bony knees, blue chin and a fantastic cap tipped over one eye, he sat nursing a heavily bandaged foot and leg, whilst he surveyed the scene before him with mournful disgust.

"Jesus Chrrrist," was all he said.

"Hullo, Scotty," hailed the "Tommy." "Come and take a seat over 'ere. Ceiling's leakin' over this part, so it's makin' the floor nice and soft to sit on." The Scot replied in his strange northern patois, but never relaxed a muscle of his face. He was excessively respectful to me when I dressed his foot, and when I addressed him in English which he apparently understood, he broke into a long and dreary story quite unintelligible to me which obviously filled him with great indignation. But while he was talking an idea entered my head. Why could I not contrive the escape of such British prisoners as were brought to the hospital by smuggling them over the frontier into Holland, which was not far distant?

It was nine o'clock next evening, and, under the moon the dim countryside stretched away a shadowy blue as I bumped back towards Roulers, while the Scot wedged between me and the ambulance driver groaned at every jolt. The Allies were "putting stuff over," and now and again a moaning shriek heralded a vivid flash and concussion in the fields to our right and left. Suddenly the air seemed palpitating, searing flame enveloped us, the wind-screen leaped from its frame into our faces, and mid a thunderous detonation, the ambulance lurched quivering to one side and turned over in the ditch. For a moment I scarcely breathed, hardly sure that I was alive, then the frantic struggling of someone on top of me who kept muttering, "Jesus Chrrrist, Jesus Chrrrist," told me that wherever I was the Scot was still with me. He dragged himself free with grunts of pain, and helped me out. The moon looked down as we gazed round the quiet landscape. A jagged hole yawned in the road. The driver—an Alsatian, named Alphonse, whom I was to know better later—had been hurled clear and lay in a dazed but otherwise unharmed condition in the road.

The medical orderly crawled from the back of the vehicle, and the three of us without a word started groping in the tumbled interior for those invisible, moaning stretcher-cases. When we brought them out into the road, one man lay limp and still. We re-adjusted the dressings of the others, then stood looking at each other wondering what we should do next. The Scot drew my attention to the fact that I was bleeding badly from the shoulder and left wrist, and I saw that both forearms were scratched and scored, because I had raised my arms to ward off the shattered glass when the explosion came. The orderly had just tied me up roughly with the aid of a first-field dressing-packet which the Scot had produced from a pocket, when the sound of distant marching reached us. Presently a silent battalion trudged past, going up the line. The adjutant stopped and inquired what had happened and ordered a cyclist to hurry to Roulers for help.

By 10.30 p.m. my charges were safely in bed in the hospital, and feeling happier than I had been for days, despite injuries and tiredness, for I felt that I had in some measure atoned for the part I had played in the terrible raid on the station, I went to the dispensary to have my hurts properly dressed. While an orderly was doing this there was a commotion in the main hall into which the dispensary opened. Two military policemen carried in a civilian who was breathing in great whistling gasps.

"Found him in a ditch, Fräulein," one of the soldiers explained, "someone has been trying to cut his throat." The man was nearly dead from loss of blood already, and I sent an orderly for the night-surgeon. Meanwhile, I tried to ease the man as much as possible. In doing this my eyes were suddenly caught by something that flashed on the inner lapel of his coat, which had been rucked up. Two steel safety-pins were fixed there. But they ran straight and not diagonally!

"Do you know who this man is?" I asked the military policemen who were standing watching.

"Yes, Fräulein," came the answer, "that's Schneider of the Police. He has been on special work for some weeks now."

When I returned home the stranger, who had rarely spoken to me since that first night, was seated, pipe in mouth, alone in the kitchen, and with feet propped up on the stove was unlacing his muddy boots.

"A 'safety-pin man,' whose pins were straight and not diagonal, was brought in with his throat cut to-night," I told him.

The stranger paused, then pulled off his boot and laid it on the fender.

"Did he die?" he inquired in a toneless voice.

CHAPTER IV

Of the normal weekly routine of transmitting unimportant information, the arrival and departure of troops, the destinations of German regiments, and the like, I shall make no mention, for it would become tedious and the reader may take it for granted. It is the more outstanding episodes of my life as a spy, which contributed toward the building of a girl's character into that of a woman and which have left their impress for ever on my mind, that concern me here.

In the middle of March, 1915, my father was offered the proprietorship of the Carillon Café by its owner who, with his family, was going to a town farther behind the lines. The café nestled in the shadow of the tall grey church of Roulers on the Grand Place, and this incidentally sheltered it to some extent from Allied shell-fire. Wide steps led up from the Grand Place to a beautiful façade of old Flemish style, and through this one passed into a large room with a counter which was used as the café. The two upper storys at the back of the house had been struck by a bomb, and were nothing but bricks, rubble, and splintered beams, but for all that, there was still ample accommodation.

My mother and I pondered for long over this offer. It certainly offered many advantages, being reasonably safe and having a spacious cellar, and the income would help the *ménage*, for the War had sadly curtailed my father's assets. Men will talk and boast over strong liquor, and men are also apt to pay attentions to the proprietress' daughter. I realized that much useful information might be picked up in this way; but on the other hand the thought "Was it too obvious?" occurred to me, and in actual practice, should I be placing myself in a prominent and dangerous position? At that time there were many exaggerated stories current among the Germans in Belgium of the "café girls," and the way they had suffered for trying to make men talk, and although I feared that these tales might throw suspicion on me, I decided that the advantages would prove worth the risk.

As I should no longer have to come in contact merely with the hospital staff, with whom I was on the best of terms, but with all kinds of officers and men who would probably frequent the café, I decided that I must have a definite attitude towards all Germans. I frequently acted as spokesman and go-between for the townspeople in their dealings with the Town-Kommandant. I was, therefore, to some extent in the good books of the authorities, and without presuming upon this or overstepping the bounds, I must above all else keep this good will. A too friendly attitude on the surface would almost certainly arouse the suspicions of the German Secret Service, who were by no means fools, but at the same time I must contrive to be popular in a detached way and to gain the confidence of the men, so that I was the very last person in the world they would suspect. I bore myself, therefore, as an aloof, rather detached girl, who was quite honestly and openly in sympathy with the Allies and the sorrows of down-trodden

Belgium, but as one nevertheless who held no ill-feeling to individual fighting men if they behaved themselves. I made a point of bestowing my smiles upon regular clients, and I arranged for washing, mending and other small jobs to be done for them—"Never encourage anybody, never speak to anybody; just let them know that you are there and wait for them to make the overtures," was the essence of my policy. I was surprised how well and in what a short while this procedure began to show results.

From the first the café was well patronized not only by the military, but also by the civilians. We kept one upstairs room which overlooked the Place as a private room to be used for dinner parties and special entertainments. When not in use for other purposes, it was employed as a lounge for officers, and at nights this was almost always full of tobacco smoke and chatter. When I was home from the hospital in the evenings I waited on our clients—with the two girls whom my mother had hired—either up or downstairs.

We had moved into the café at the beginning of March, and it was about one week later when I returned from the hospital earlier than usual that Bertha, one of our girls, approached with a very long face and told me there were three German officers not long arrived, who had announced their intention of billeting upon us. This was the last thing I had wanted, as I was afraid it might curtail my activities, but it could not be helped. The lounge had not yet filled up, and when the hand-bell rang I went upstairs to ask for orders, anxious to see what sort of men were to live in the house with us.

Three officers sat round the oak table in the centre of the room gazing over empty wine glasses. They had flung their equipment in a pile on the floor. Two Hauptmanns leaned back with tunics undone, and puffed cigars. The other, a fair young lieutenant, very neat and tightly buttoned up, watched me with elbows on table and chin on hands.

When I had brought the wine they ordered, the large, florid Hauptmann with red hair raised his glass.

"Fräulein, won't you do us the honour to drink a glass with us?" he started, rising to his feet. "Drink to our trip to Paris." He looked across at the others in a knowing way.

"Thank you, Herr, but I have had a very tiring day at the hospital, and there are times when I do not feel that I want a drink." I was, to say the least of it, intrigued with that queer look he had flashed to the other two officers when he mentioned the "trip to Paris." It was perhaps a merely fatuous remark, but that acute, inexplicable sense of being on the track of a secret was beginning to develop in me even in those early days.

"So you are from the hospital on the Menin Road?" rumbled the red-haired man as though I had committed some crime.

"Yes, Herr."

"Really, Red Carl," said a cherubic young voice, "you haven't been sent here to court-martial this lady, you know." I noticed the speaker's wavy golden hair and his lively eyes. He certainly was an attractive boy.

The other Hauptmann, a long cadaverous man of about middle age with hair so closely cropped that his head appeared shaved, examined me through his large spectacles with a cold smile.

"Perhaps the Fräulein will be kind enough to show us where are our sleeping quarters," he suggested in a strangely quiet voice. There was something intense and queer about this man which made one feel he was very dangerous, although in what way he could make himself particularly dangerous I could not imagine.

They followed me silently. I was going to give the spectacled Hauptmann a room to himself as he was obviously the senior, and give our remaining room to be shared between the other two. But the spectacled one turned to me:

"Fräulein," he said, "I shall share with the Herr Hauptmann. We two have work that we must carry out together." His eyes glinted behind his glasses. "The Herr Lieutenant can take my room."

"Splendid," chuckled the lieutenant. "Red Carl, if you snore as thunderously to-night as you did with me in the train last night, I think at Hauptmann Reichmann's hands you will die a nasty, sticky death."

"Oh no—you wouldn't kill me, would you, you sinister old devil," grunted Red Carl, putting his arm good-humouredly about Reichmann's skinny neck. "I'm too damned valuable to you, eh?" I showed the two into their room, and then went back to the lieutenant who had called to me.

"Queer couple, those two, aren't they, Fräulein? Possibly you think them a trifle rude and surly, but they don't mean to be. Just like brothers, and always wrapped up in their own ideas."

"Yes," I agreed. "What are they?" I had noticed that neither of the Hauptmanns were of the Army of Würtemburg, and that they wore the badges of some special unit which I did not recognize.

"Just two representatives whom we have sent ahead to arrange our 'trip to Paris,'" he laughed. I knew it would be imprudent for me to say anything further, but there was some mystery here which needed probing.

In his room, the lieutenant, who told me that his name was Otto Von Promft, threw himself on to the bed, and lighted an expensive cigarette after offering me the case.

"You were a student, I see," I remarked.

"So you noticed my duelling scar," he responded with pride. "I left Stuttgart six months ago."

Then he suddenly broke into fluent French. He told me he had lived in Paris most of his life until the War.

"I have been in various parts of Belgium," he told me during our conversation. "Everywhere it is the custom of you Belgians to bewail the terrible conditions under which you are forced to live, but I have recently returned from leave, and I daresay you will be surprised to hear that in our capital the regulations are just as great as those that you know in Belgium." He went on to paint a distressing picture with which I could sympathize, and was absolutely frank in all he said.

"However," he finished, "we Germans know how to put up with a lot, so it does not greatly matter. We are bound to win."

"You may win great victories, but I do not believe that in the end you will emerge from this War the victors," I observed.

"Fräulein, as yet Germany is not even tried. A victory, a sudden overwhelming, crushing victory is coming, and it is coming soon." Some officers came up and rang the bell in the front room, so I told Otto I must go. Altogether we had been talking about half an hour. Those eyes of his somehow made you feel that he genuinely liked you.

Since the day I had worked in the advanced dressing-station I had become very good friends with the two wounded British prisoners, the Highlander and the talkative one with the cigarette who had been in the dugout. They both belonged to Canadian units. Jimmie was a common little man, originally emanating from a London slum. He possessed all the rough wit and good-humour of his class and was always cheerful. He made a joke when we had to put him on the operating table, and followed it with another one before he was violently sick when he woke up after we had done with him. I eventually found that I was able to understand the Highlander's patois. He had been a miner in civil life, and was self-educated, with a serious argumentative outlook on life. He had taught himself quite a fair knowledge of French, and I used to lend him books in that language. One night he confessed to me in confidence:

"It has always bin ma weish, leddie, if a' could but acquirre the learmin', to become a meenister." His meaning rather puzzled me at first, but when I understood, I could not help laughing at the thought of this gaunt giant who decorated his every tenth word with "Jesus Chrrist" ministering to his flock in a black suit. His name was Arthur.

One morning, as was not uncommon, I entered the ward to hear Jimmie and Arthur in fierce dispute.

"Have ye no bin to schule, mun—do ye know nothing?" expostulated Arthur mournfully at his grinning mate, who had just remarked something about a "Bleeding Liar."

"Arthur."

At my whisper he turned his head. I had slipped close to his bed. An eager look lighted his face. We had often talked together in the hospital grounds, while they were taking their daily airing, and I had hinted at assisting them to escape. On the pretext of tucking in his sheets I whispered rapidly: "Here are a thousand francs for you and Jimmie. When you are walking in the grounds this evening look out for a small Belgian with a squint near the civilian workers' annexe. Slip through the door. You will find clothes. Trust your guide; he will get you over the border."

Then I was gone, leaving Arthur gaping. Both of them were in the convalescent stage, their wounds having healed without trouble, and I could never understand why they had not already been evacuated. The thousand francs was all I could raise at the moment, but Pierre—the Belgian civilian—would also help. The rest of the day I was on tenterhooks. Had I left a clue by which, should the lads be caught, I could be traced? I knew they would never betray me no matter what happened; but of Pierre I was not so certain.

Before the War he had been known as one of the worst characters in Roulers. He was always drunk, rarely did any work, and had been to prison numberless times for petty theft. Now he worked as one of the civilian employees about the hospital. He was a cheery old ruffian with a squint eye, and it was he who had broached the idea of prisoners escaping when I spoke to him while he was pruning rose bushes in the garden a fortnight before. His sly look and his swivel eye had frightened me, and as he could show no safety-pins, I hurried away pretending to take no notice. Arthur had told me that the old man had also approached him, speaking in a mixture of halting English and French, but had told him that he could not help them alone because he had not the money. The man might be a cunning counter-espionage agent of the Germans, but after a lot of thought I had decided to take this risk.

Soon after leaving the two Canadians, a wire came through that two ambulance convoys were to be expected, and in the rush of work the matter slipped from my mind. At six o'clock I went off duty, ate a hasty meal and tried to read. The printed words swam meaninglessly in front of me. It must have been eight o'clock when there was a sudden ringing of bells from the hospital. Men were shouting, running, waving their arms.

I hurried over to my ward. Jimmie's bed was empty. So was Arthur's. A Feldwebel rushed in.

"What do you know of this, nurse?" he roared. "Two patients from your ward walk off right under your nose! Disgraceful! When did you see them last? Have they got civilian clothes or money?"

I professed complete ignorance of the whole affair. I had been off duty and had seen nothing. Presently I managed to slip into the civilians' annexe, where the workmen lived and those assisting in ambulance work. In the doorway I met a man I had never seen before, a big, bearded fellow with flaxen hair.

"Good evening, Little Mother," he said, giving me the name by which I was known amongst the townsfolk. "A friend of mine asked me to give you a message. His friends are leaving and will be in Holland by midnight!"

I breathed again. The squint-eyed Pierre had done the trick. I thanked him and went home to bed, but found two men waiting for me in our sitting-room. My mother was busy in the kitchen.

"Alphonse—Stephan?" I ejaculated in surprise. "What is this? Am I wanted at the hospital?"

Alphonse, the Alsatian, had been pressed into the German Army to drive an ambulance. He was a short, thick-set man who had been training in a seminary for the priesthood when he was conscripted. It was he who had driven me that night I went up to the advanced dressing-station, and since then we had often chatted together. Stephan, his friend, was a Pole employed as a clerk in the Brigade Orderly Room, and appeared rather a delicate young man with a moustache. They were both eyeing me queerly now. Could they be German agents? I was a fool not to have connected them with the counter-espionage work, and now they had got me over the affair of this escape. The palms of my hands grew clammy at the thought. The game was up.

"Alphonse has cut his finger repairing the engine of his car. Nothing serious, but—as we were passing—" explained Stephan quietly.

"Of course," I said, my heart beating wildly. "Of course I will dress it for him. Sit down, won't you, while I fetch my bandages?"

I ran upstairs in an agony of apprehension. How long had they been in the house? Why had they called? Stephan could have dressed the cut himself, *if indeed it required dressing*. Had they really discovered my double job? All these questions and a hundred others hammered at my brain as I picked up my little work-basket and my bandages.

Stephan was sitting on the table when I got back, Alphonse was looking at the pictures on the walls. I tried to persuade myself that everything was all right, that their visit was after all perfectly natural, and yet it was only with a great effort that I managed to steady myself and appear quite unperturbed.

"Now, Stephan," I said, "where is this cut?"

"How do you like your double job, sister?" he suddenly said as I was bending over a small gash on his finger that he might well have bandaged himself. I went as pale as death, but kept my head down so that he could not observe me and, clenching my teeth, willed my hands not to tremble.

"Perhaps you would like a pin to fasten the bandage?" he remarked, "I have a safety-pin."

My heart bounded with joy, but I still had to be cautious.

"Have you a small one handy?" I inquired.

He lifted the lapel of his great-coat showing two diagonal safety-pins. I smiled with relief and turned up the collar of my nurse's uniform. Alphonse copied Stephan. Then we re-hid the fateful pins in silence.

"So you see, sister, we all have pins, and we all serve Belgium together, eh?"

"How did you get to know how I was employed?" I asked.

"The sergeant-major of the canteen told us to visit you, sister."

"What," I gasped horrified. "That German——"

"He is not a German," said Alphonse. "Not so many years ago that sergeant was a cadet at the Military College of Sandhurst, England. He was sent to Germany before the War."

"And he sent you to me?"

"Until yesterday he was our channel of communication, but unfortunately he has been transferred elsewhere. Stephan works at Brigade H.Q., so you can understand he sometimes learns things that are interesting, and as I myself frequently have to go to the line, I also manage to pick up a thing or two.—We were told that we must hand our messages to 'Laura,' and when we knew who 'Laura' was, you could have knocked us down with a feather."

"You have information for me?"

"First of all, sister, let us speak of another matter." It was the pale Stephan who was speaking, as he nervously fingered one end of his moustache. "There is, I understand, billeted in this café at present a young officer called Otto von Promft?"

"That is so."

"You like him?"

"What has that to do with you? He is a nice straightforward boy, and better than most Germans."

"That is where you are wrong, sister," drawled Stephan, shaking his head grimly. "The charming Otto has been sent to live in your café as a decoy."

"How do you know that?—Then they suspect me?" I felt myself trembling.

"Not necessarily, sister; the Germans suspect all Belgians unless they are imbeciles or on their death-beds. However, there is a chance of this, and it will be necessary for you to be very watchful.—I will tell you how I discovered about this Otto. It is one of my duties at Brigade H.Q. to assist the Censor officer if he is particularly busy. I open the letters and place them before him, and then close them for posting. Sometimes the Censor arrives late, and always takes a long time over his meals. It is not therefore difficult for me to find opportunity for reading many letters, often before the Censor himself has attacked them with his chalk.—The mail of officers usually arrives at H.Q. in separate packages, and these I naturally consider most likely to yield matter of value.—It was last week that in one of these packets, I came upon the letter of a certain Otto von Promft. He was telling his mother that the special work upon which they had sent him to Roulers was both easy and interesting, allowing him much leisure, and that if he were successful in his mission as he hoped in the end he would be, he might be able to find a 'cushy' job in Berlin. This was interesting and unusual, and after careful inquiry I found that this officer lived at a café, was very friendly with everybody, and was employed neither regimentally, nor by the police, in any normal branch of the staff."

"I am more than grateful to you," I assured him, mentally stabbing the deceitful Otto a thousand times to death. I was not so much frightened of him at that moment, as furiously indignant with him for having made me like him. "And now what of the information you have for me to pass on?"

"Perhaps we might have some wine over which to discuss it, sister, for it is a puzzler I can assure you," said Alphonse, tickling the back of his close-cropped head thoughtfully. I went to fetch the wine, and at the foot of the stairs came face to face with deceitful Otto who was going up to the officers' lounge. He bowed and saluted with his most disarming smile, and I gave him that gracious and melting look he expected.

"I hope you will find time to have a drink with me later, Fräulein," he invited.

"Not to-night, Herr Otto," I excused myself. "I am tired, but to-morrow perhaps." It is strange that when you know the true character of a person, the face often seems to change from that which you have previously known. It had happened with Otto. The boyish lineaments appeared to have given place to a cunning, foxy expression. However, I had got to continue being as friendly with him as ever, hoping that he did not and would not suspect.

Upstairs Stephan began to talk. In the last ammunition train to arrive, besides the usual freight, were several trucks containing long metal cylinders. He had not been able by any means to find out for what they were intended, and he did not think many of the Germans knew themselves. "Whatever they are," he said, "I think perhaps a bomb would do them a bit of good, so the sooner you can inform the British that these are waiting in the station, the better."

"I shall send them information to-night," I assured him. "Meanwhile, do your utmost to find out from Brigade what these cylinders contain."

"I, too, have some unusual information for you, sister. Yesterday afternoon, when I should normally have been off duty, I and another ambulance driver were sent on several trips to and from the station, bringing great bales of cotton-wool swabs to the hospital store. These were not dressing-pads for wounds, as they had pieces of elastic fixed to them.—I have never seen anything like them before."

"Was there no sort of descriptive label on the bale, as is usual with military stores?"

"Yes, and this is even stranger. They were not addressed to the C.O. of the hospital, or even to any officer of the medical corps. The label simply said that they were to be held at the disposal of a certain Hauptmann Reichmann."

"Hauptmann Reichmann," I ejaculated in astonishment. "He is billeted here."

"Yes. Stephan discovered that from the Brigade register; but he appears to belong to no unit and nothing there is known about him——"

"But he has three times visited Brigade, and had long private conferences with the Brigadier," broke in Stephan.

"Sister, I think you should take every opportunity of watching this officer, for he is obviously a man of some importance, although I cannot for the life of me see in what way!"

Not long after the two of them bid me "Good night," after we had agreed that in future only two of us must ever be together at the same time, and that we must not seem to be anything but casual acquaintances to outsiders.

It was late and all our clients had left, some a trifle noisily, for their sleeping quarters, for many of them were not blessed with beds. There was no point in informing the British about our cadaverous guest Reichmann until I knew more, as there might be nothing in the matter, but I described the arrival of the cylinders as precisely as possible in code, and putting the message in my hair, slipped down the darkened stairs to the silence of the streets. From the far side of the Place the gruff voices of the patrol and the clink of metal reached me. It was very dark, and presently I came to the silent alleyway which harboured the mysterious No. 63. At the fifth window on the left-hand side, I tapped according to the signal—once—a pause, then twice rapidly. The frame slid up without a sound, and the hand appeared. Into it I pushed my notes and then sped out of the alley as if the devil was behind me. An hour later I was asleep, dreaming that I had been taken and was being court-martialled by the Oberartz.

A few mornings later I saw Canteen Ma in the Grand Place, surrounded by laughing soldiers, giving a joke and some good-humoured chaff, all the while speaking her impossible German. All the Germans loved her and would greet her familiarly, and she found them ready purchasers. She was just wiping her lips with the back of her hand as I passed, after a mug of beer to which somebody had treated her from our café, and as she was going in my direction, she shouted after me, and then said quietly:

"Martha, there is something in the air here. There is too much talk of a sweeping victory among the men for things to be normal, yet none of them knows anything."

That same evening Stephan gave me the first piece in the jig-saw puzzle. He said that Reichmann had started sending in weather reports to Brigade twice a day. The variations of the wind were graphed. The districts were the Roulers-Menin and Poelcappele-Passchendaele Roads. Red Carl had several times been up in an aeroplane to take observations and twice in the observation balloon on the Menin Road. I came to the conclusion that Reichmann might have some papers in his room which could give us some clue, and accordingly I asked my mother, who made his bed every morning, to keep her eyes open. She told me that Reichmann filed duplicate copies of the strange graphs on his table, and that he was also keeping a sort of log of the weather. I determined to see for myself. Accordingly I sent to the hospital, saying I was unwell, the next morning, and when I knew that Reichmann, Carl and Otto had all gone out, crept from my bedroom into Reichmann's and examined the documents on his table. Sure enough there was the weather log and the wind graphs, but there was nothing else. I left the room as mystified as I went in. But that night I informed the British by the hand of No. 63 about the mysterious wind graphs.

Two days later Canteen Ma called at the door and the pin-cushion she left contained the following message:

"Do not worry about weather reports. Troop movements, designation of units, trains, etc., of more value."

But for all that I did continue to worry. And that night I found myself going to bed even more puzzled.

Red Carl was sitting at a corner of the smoky lounge by himself. He looked slightly the worse for drink, wanted someone to talk to, so he beckoned me across.

"Have you ever been to Germany, Fräulein," he started, offering me a cigarette and lighting it with a rather shaky hand.

"No, Herr."

"You do not like the Germans, hein?"

"Well, you could not expect us to exactly love them after this shambles. Eh, Herr?"

"Ach—well never mind, Fräulein. Even if we don't succeed in winning the War soon, we shall have pushed so far into France that Roulers will hardly know a German soldier except patrols. Nach Paris! Nach Calais!" He banged his empty beer-glass so hard down on the table that I was surprised it did not smash. Then ensued a little pause while he sat dreaming heroically in a mirage of alcoholic glory.

"You Germans are good at telling that sort of story. I could tell you the names of several Germans who used to say 'Nach Paris! Nach Calais!' last year!"

"Aha—maybe, but I am in the know," he chuckled in his deep way. "Yes, it's funny. Damned funny! Blasted funny! Here am I, Carl Sturme, despised chemist, a man whom these snobs of generals with their choker collars and their eyeglasses would in the old days have regarded with as much respect as they did the paving-stones under their feet, but who is now going to play a bigger hand in winning the mightiest war the world has ever known than they themselves, for all their swaggering militarism."—Then he went on chuckling to himself till some friends came in, when he wandered over to them, and kept them laughing with a continual flow of tipsy bragging for the rest of the evening. So Red Carl was a chemist, had no sort of ordinary military job, and he had boasted in his cups about a great victory of which he was cocksure, and bubbled a string of disgruntled nonsense. But there is always a grain of sense among the chaff, I told myself as I went to bed, racking my brains for what it would all mean.

The following day I managed to find an opportunity to tell both Stephan and Alphonse what Carl had said the night before. Alphonse thought that Carl had invented some new type of artillery, and that his calculations and graphs had something to do with this. Stephan suggested that if there was to be a great advance in this area, as was apparently the case, they might be considering Roulers as a Zeppelin base. I did not feel satisfied with either of these suppositions, but decided to mention both of them in my report to the British. Alphonse had another piece of news for me. He said he had been told by a man in charge of the dump of metal cylinders that they contained chlorine, but still he did not know what they were for. I was not, as a matter of fact, at that moment, inclined to pay much attention to these cylinders.

On the way home, however, the analogy between "chemist" and "chlorine" suddenly struck me. Could Red Carl have anything to do with those cylinders? Red Carl had said strange things, and then there was the "chemist–chlorine" idea. Perhaps it seemed a trifle far-fetched, but that night I reported that the wind graphs were still being compiled with regularity, the suggestions as to their use, and my idea about Carl and the chlorine cylinders. It was my job to report every happening I thought of significance. The British Intelligence might be more successful than I in understanding them.

Three days later came a message:

"Recent reports of yours of a highly speculative nature. Repeat, troop movements, designation of units, trains, etc., of more value."

So they evidently thought me just a rather foolish, imaginative girl who made mountains out of molehills.

The weather watchers continued to put in their reports day by day, and I made one new discovery. I talked to the gaunt Reichmann one evening, and drew him on to talk of his life in pre-War days, and his home. He had been a professor of a big university. It was not difficult to guess what he had been a professor of, when one remembered his association with Carl and, a fact which I subsequently noticed, that he regularly received periodicals by home mail which were of a scientific character.

The thought of "victory before the summer" seemed to have become an obsession among the Germans. The inspired press helped matters on, and grotesque, ribald and indecent cartoons, depicting Allied soldiers in all kinds of degrading situations, decorated every newspaper.

One morning in early April I reached the hospital to find it full of bustle. All possible cases that could be moved were to be evacuated at once. A medical station for civilians was to be opened in the town itself so as to relieve the hospital of this branch of work, which was sometimes considerable.

"Ah, Fräulein," greeted the Oberartz in his genial voice, "I think we are in for an advance. All stations this side of Ghent have been warned to evacuate their wounded immediately." Repressing my burning interest I remained silent, expecting to hear some further information, but he passed on without any other remark. This was important news. Evacuation from hospitals close up to the line meant advance. I got my report away to No. 63 that night. Then I anxiously watched for the flood of reinforcements. But day followed day, and no further troops arrived. The 26th and 27th Corps of the Würtemburg Army held the sector, front and reserve lines.

The Army carried out its own reliefs as usual, not an extra gun or an extra soldier passed up the line. I was completely mystified. In talking the conundrum over with Alphonse he thought perhaps it might mean a feint at this part of the salient to cover some determined assault at another point. Still, I had grave misgivings. In any case, I had done my utmost. I had faithfully recorded every possible clue to the riddle, which had come under my notice. And a short week later the solution fell with a blinding crash.

The 22nd of April, 1915, I well remember was a beautiful day with gentle spring breezes bringing promise of summer, but from the slopes of the Passchendaele Ridges another kind of breeze—"a Devil's Wind"—had been slowly creeping over "No Man's Land," enveloping the Allied trenches at Langemarck and about Poelcappele in a mysterious haze of death.

Soon after it grew light on the morning of the 23rd, I received an urgent message from the hospital to be in attendance immediately. I hurried there and almost at once the stream of ambulances with the unfortunate prisoners began to arrive. At first scores, then later hundreds of broken men, gasping, screaming, choking. The hospital was packed with French soldiers, beating and fighting the air for breath. Dozens of men were dying like flies, their clothes rent to ribbons in their agony, their faces a horrible sickly green and contorted out of all human shape. Tunics and brass buttons had also turned green, and a pungent suffocating smell hung around them. When no more room could be found along the hospital corridors, the stretcher-bearers laid them out on the foot paths and the streets surrounding the building.—"What is it?—What is it?" kept pounding in my brain—"What Devil's work is this?"—as I worked amid that hellish scene striving to soothe and quieten the stricken. Still the ambulances full of prisoners came, and more and more forms struggled and tossed in the roadway. My heart bleeding with pity, I bent over a young British soldier, a Canadian, and whispered: "What has happened, brother?" He looked up with inflamed swollen eyes almost bursting from the sockets, but he could not speak, only painfully shake his head as he propped himself on his arms, coughing and spitting.

As the number of prisoners grew, the civilian population had gathered at both ends of the street. A section of German soldiers were keeping them back with their rifles. Suddenly a voice from the crowd cried, "Vive la France"—"Vive l'Angleterre," and then the cry burst from every throat till it swelled to a mad indignant uproar. Even the poor gassed prisoners tried to sit up and join in the cry of "Vive la France"—"Vive l'Angleterre." That is a moment that will for ever remain in my memory. Blinded with tears, the people showered cigarettes, bread and chocolate on the stricken soldiers: although God knows where it came from, for we were all fearfully short and hungry in those days. The soldiers were being forced back by the savage crowd. Then suddenly came the clatter of hooves and a *posse* of mounted gendarmes trotted up the road. They put their horses' heads into the crowd and started to force them away.—The riddle of the wind graphs had been answered.

It is for the historian to tell how the line was shattered and bent, how near the Germans were to a crushing victory, but how the comrades of those stricken wretches, who could still cry out "Vive la France"—"Vive l'Angleterre," withstood the shock, and desperately won their way back through a hell of carnage. Nor will the historian forget those heroic victims who died under the first gas attack.

~

Throughout this history of my life during the War years it is my aim to deal with events in the order in which they actually happened, but in order to make the riddle of the wind graphs a continuous narrative, I passed over a strange incident which occurred in the café some ten days before the first gas attack.

Owing to the mysterious evacuation of wounded from the hospital it had been left largely empty and I was allowed much time off. It was half-past four as I reached the café steps, for I remember looking at my watch. The skies were gloomy and a cold wind rustled the dust of the almost deserted Place. There were no Germans in the front lower room, for they did not usually arrive till later, but there were ten civilians, two women and the rest men.

Leaning over the counter chatting with my mother was the mysterious stranger. Since we had left our old lodgings I had occasionally seen him about the streets, and he had several times visited the café, when he appeared to be on friendly terms with several of the Germans present. He always greeted me in a friendly way, but he had never spoken confidentially since we had come to the café. I had heard several instances of German plain-clothes agents disappearing unaccountably, but the world was full of strange rumours in those days. I approached the counter and the stranger nodded, then seeing that there was nobody likely to overhear, he said in an undertone:

"I have decided to go elsewhere, for I think it is likely to get hot for me here before long. Yesterday the German agents visited the house and examined my passport, seeming to be very suspicious although they could find nothing wrong with it. My landlady tells me also that the Germans in the house have been asking questions." Glancing round I saw a Hauptmann come in, one of our regular customers. I gave the stranger a warning look. The officer strode to the counter, ordered cigarettes and chatted pleasantry with my mother. A few moments later the door again swung open and the Lieutenant of Military Police stood in the doorway who had been present when I had undergone that first terrifying interrogation in the kitchen of our old lodging. The officer wore a stern look on his face as he stood by the door surveying the inmates of the café. His eyes fixed on the back of a middle-aged Belgian, who sat at a table in the centre of the room by himself. I had never spoken to him, and did not know who he was, although I had sometimes seen him about the town. He was rough and burly, as if he might be a small farmer who did much of his own work. I saw the officer frown and purse his lips. Then he approached and stood looking at him.

"You are not a native of Roulers," he interrogated sharply. "I should like to see your passport."

The man regarded him calmly and produced the document from an inner pocket. The Lieutenant perused it, seemed annoyed at its correctness, then tossed it back. The man began to refold it. Suddenly the military policeman caught the lapel of his jacket and jerked it upright. Beneath were two safety-pins running diagonally.

The German chuckled grimly in the silence which had fallen on the room.

"I think you had better come along with me," he growled quietly, dragging the man violently to his feet. The stranger had remained leaning over the counter watching this unusual act without stirring a muscle. Suddenly he straightened. He walked up to the German officer.

"I wish to speak to you, Herr," he said. The German regarded him with surprise.

"Well, what do you want?"

The stranger's back was to me as he faced the officer, but suddenly I saw his right arm jerk forcefully upwards, and I heard his hiss, "Raoul, take the back door and make for the frontier."

The stranger had moved to one side and the German stood there deathly pale, supporting himself with convulsive fingers around the table edge. Protruding from his left breast was the hilt of a large knife. He tottered for a moment, then his eyes rolled, showing the white, and he crumpled in a heap to the floor. Like a flash Raoul turned and sped through into the kitchen before the Hauptmann at the counter had grasped what had happened. He saw the stranger still standing in the middle of the room, and with an oath blundered towards him. Picking up a bottle off the table, the stranger waited the assault, then darting to one side at the last minute, he struck the officer unconscious with his bottle. He put the bottle back quietly on the table, swallowed the untasted half of the wine in Raoul's glass, and walked out of the house without a word, since nobody wanted to stop him. He was never seen in Roulers again.

To have had a German police officer murdered in our café in broad daylight would have proved serious for all of us in the place at the time if the Hauptmann had not come from hospital to testify at the harsh examination which followed that the whole incident was entirely unexpected and none of us had taken any hand. When asked why they had not apprehended the murderer, the men all vowed that he had threatened them with a revolver, and as the Hauptmann, being unconscious at the time, could not contradict them, this had to be accepted for the truth.

CHAPTER V

For about a week in the beginning of May Roulers had a bad time. A group of seven British aeroplanes, nicknamed by the Germans the "Seven Sisters," flew over the town and bombed us every night. Shells frequently crashed into the streets and the houses, and at times aeroplanes swept low over the main thoroughfares in broad daylight, machine-gunning all within sight below.

The German Intelligence authorities were well aware that Roulers, and other towns like it near the line, supplied a great deal of valuable information to the enemy, but they were finding spies difficult to catch. I knew that they had been anxious for some time to evacuate the civilian populations from all the areas near the line, but had hesitated to do so for fear of the Allied propaganda bureaux, which would un-doubtedly make the most of such a splendid opportunity for attacking the Hun in regard to his brutal methods with innocent civilians. Now that Roulers had become an exceedingly dangerous place, it was thought that the Germans might use this as a good excuse for sending civilians out of the town. All Belgians had already been forced to leave the large village of Staden for that reason, and the rumour became widespread both among the civilians and the troops in Roulers, that the civilians were to leave the place for farther inland.

Several relations of mine used to live in Staden and one of these, an uncle, was permitted to take his family to a farm which he owned at Ruddervoorde, towards the coast on the route to Brugge, when the authorities issued the order for evacuation.

I received a request through Canteen Ma to obtain what information I could about conditions round the Brugge coast district. This district was guarded with the utmost vigilance by the German Marine Corps, and almost a reign of terror existed, civilians being flung into prison on the faintest suspicions, and even the mention of the word "spy" meaning a firing party. So far none of the inhabitants of the area had succeeded in getting over information to the Allies, for they were all watched, searched, examined and reported on too carefully, but they had abandoned the attempt. It was wondered, therefore, whether someone from outside might manage to gain the wanted information.

The second clause in the message from Canteen Ma ran as follows: "Important information is regularly leaking through to the enemy. From certain information which has come to hand through interrogation of German prisoners, etc., we have learnt that a concealed telephone line runs from some unknown location behind the British lines to a terminating point situated in the wooded area about Ruddervoorde, Brugge district. Unable to find termination our side of line. Information regarding site of this telephone line and identity of operator behind British line urgently needed."

At first the whole idea seemed hopeless. True, my uncle lived in Ruddervoorde, but to penetrate there and return by clandestine means, or even to get a pass which would allow me to return, seemed, I frankly admitted to myself, impossible. It would have been simpler to go to the Congo. Then the strength of the rumour about the evacuation of Roulers by civilians gave me an idea. It was rather wild and far-fetched, and had several "ifs" about it, but still it was an idea and it might work.

Soon after the first and second gas attacks the two sinister chemists had left their billets in our café and a Hauptmann Fashugel, a machine-gun company commander, was occupying their room. Otto still remained with us, a friend and yet an enemy, the very sight of whom sent a shiver of apprehension down my spine, for I never knew whether he suspected me or not, but I had no choice except to carry on with my job. We also had now three sergeants who slept on straw in the cellar. Hauptmann Fashugel had been recovering from wounds in the hospital when I first went there and we had become good friends. He was a big dashing fellow, in appearance reminiscent of that famous portrait, "The Laughing Cavalier." His men loved him for his wildness and because he knew how to joke with them at times, despite the fact that he was very foul-mouthed and treated them harshly.

One evening in the street I was hailed by Fashugel, very dusty and tired and slung about with equipment. He had just returned from a spell up the line, and having disposed of his command was making his way to the café. Now my scheme centred round Hauptmann Fashugel and when I unexpectedly heard his cheerful voice my heart gave a sudden leap. I got coffee for him in the back room when we reached the house, and he produced a rather unappetizing black-looking cake—Roulers' wartime best—and some canteen rye biscuits, which we devoured together while he told me how he loathed the War in a tone which made one feel that he rather enjoyed it.

"Have you heard the rumour which is flying about everywhere here, that all we civilians are to be sent away from Roulers?" I asked him, and he nodded. "It will be most unpleasant for us, this move," I went on.

"Well, myself, I think you will be very lucky if you get your marching orders from Roulers. There are lots of better spots than this hole."

"You forget," I said, "that when we unfortunate civilians get the order to go we have to quit immediately. No time is given us to pack our belongings, and as we can't hang them all round our belts as you do, and we very likely can't obtain any transport for them, they will have to be abandoned." He sat munching his black cake thoughtfully.

"If you have to move, to where are you thinking of going?" he put at length.

"I have an uncle who owns a farm at Ruddervoorde, so we should go there."

The German machine-gun companies at that time were self-contained units with their own transport, and owing to the great value placed upon them by the authorities, the M.-G. company commanders were allowed to go their own way far more than most other officers. And it was in this fact that I had seen my chance.

"Well," offered Fashugel, "I don't see why I couldn't lend you a wagon. Have the things waiting to be loaded at the back of the café at dusk to-morrow evening. Now where is this farm to which my driver is to deliver the stuff?"

"I am afraid he is going to find it very difficult to locate," I informed him. "It lies off a side road among trees, and there are many trees around Brugge. I don't think he would ever find it without stopping to inquire several times."

"Hm, that might be awkward," he growled, biting his lip. "You understand, Martha, that to use our transport for such a purpose is forbidden, and that I only consider it as a favour— A German wagon driver inquiring for a Belgian farmer might lead to questions which would get me into trouble———"

"It would not be possible for me to travel with him?" I suggested brightly. "I should love to see Uncle Jules again. It would be splendid if you could manage it."

"There is certainly no question of my getting a pass for you," retorted Fashugel, regarding the carpet thoughtfully, and my heart sank. "However," he smiled brightly, making a gesture with his hands. "You shall go, all the same. I have had a great brain wave, but I'll bet that you will never guess what it is."

"Tell me," I urged.

"You shall go as a German soldier, Martha," he informed me. And when he saw his suggestion had somewhat taken my breath away: "Oh, it will be all right. There is nothing to worry about. Some other man would in the normal course of events go with the driver. So who could be better than you, eh?—You are tall, and with a pair of 'pipes,' an overcoat and a forage cap, even your own Uncle Jules will mistake you for a 'knub.'"

"I think it a bit risky," I said. "Still, I'll do it if you will send me the uniform, and what is just as important, a decent reliable man as driver."

"Martha, I'll send you the quietest and best man in the whole German Army. He won't speak two words to you on the whole journey, but I'll give him orders to bring you back safely, and by God, I know 'Silent Willy' will do it."

∾

I had no exact plan in my mind as to what I was going to do when I reached the forbidden area. I wanted all possible information of the Brugge district, and I wanted also to find the site of the supposed telephone terminal. I could only wait and watch with every sense keyed so that no opportunity slipped by me. I might need to defend myself, but I could certainly not go armed. Next morning I seized a moment when I was alone to pocket a small bottle of chloroform from a hospital cupboard, as it seemed to me a good sort of weapon for a woman who would probably be overpowered in a hand to hand struggle with a man. I got leave from the Oberartz for twenty-four hours, telling him that an officer billeted with us was kindly arranging for me to take some of our valuables to a relation, but giving no details.

It was just growing dusk the next evening when I heard a wagon rumble to a standstill in the quiet lane which separated the café from the grey church walls. The driver clambered down from his high-hooded seat, and touching his cap handed me a parcel in silence. It contained a "knub's" clumsy boots and a stained and much worn uniform and greatcoat. My father helped "Silent Willy" to load the belongings on the wagon. We had naturally retained everything necessary to keep the café going, and ourselves in comfort, but some valuable *objets d'art*, some good linen in coffers, quite unobtainable then and likely to be confiscated by the Germans, and some unwanted furniture which had come to us with the café.

Meanwhile, I donned my ill-assorted military wardrobe in the back room with haste. It had obviously been collected from different owners, for the tunic was skin-tight and trousers much too baggy. Fortunately the round cap was large enough for me to coil my hair round the crown of my head in thin plaits, and as the boots and great-coat fitted pretty well, I did

MYSELF ON THE OUTBREAK OF WAR

AUGUST 1914. REFUGEES AT WESTROOSEBEKE

THE COMING OF THE GREY WAVE

CHRISTMAS 1914

MYSELF, FROM MY GERMAN OFFICIAL PASS, 1915

WEST SIDE OF THE GRAND PLACE, ROULERS, IN ITS
RESTORED STATE TODAY, SHOWING SITE OF THE CAFÉ
CARILLON

THE RUINED STATION AT ROULERS

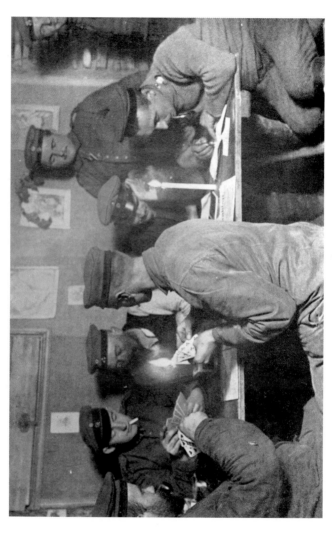

A CORNER OF THE CAFÉ AT THE BUSY HOUR

not look such a bad "knub," except for my soft cheeks and pale skin. Presently I was seated beside "Silent Willy," trundling out of Roulers behind the jingling horses. He was a burly man with a great black moustache, which he frequently swept with his hand, and very blue eyes. He showed not the slightest surprise or interest in my military rôle, and kept silence.

Several times gendarme patrols on bicycles passed us in the darkness. As we were clattering into Lichtervelde my companion mutely handed me a cheroot. I understood, for in the town there were lights in places and many soldiers were about the streets and the glow of a cigar would look better. I got it alight with the help of "Silent Willy," but after a few puffs of the black weed I began to feel sick and dizzy. Not to disappoint "Silent Willy," however, I held the offensive thing in the wind hoping that the current would keep it alight. Later on he made a gesture towards me offering another one, which I hurriedly refused.

Now and again a sentry's challenge halted us in towns or villages, and this grew more frequent as we came into a countryside where thick, dark masses of trees stood out, and the lonely silhouettes of old châteaux rose gaunt on each side. "Silent Willy's" growling reply—"The 52nd Machine-gun Company"—carried us past most sentries successfully; in fact the word "machine-gun" seemed to be an Open Sesame. But at one post two blue-clad marines came out into the centre of the road with a lantern, and "Silent Willy" had to pull up, muttering ferociously in my ear, "Blast the fools." Although my heart was palpitating with fear, I remember distinctly that I thought how funny it was that those were the only words he had addressed to me during the whole trip.

The two marines took little notice of us. They hurried round to the back of the wagon, swarmed up and began to loosen the cover which was over our belongings. Suddenly "Silent Willy" stood up on the high seat and turning roared: "Did you hear me say we were the 52nd Machine-gun Company. Isn't that enough for you?—GET OFF!!" There was such a savage steely glint in his eyes as he spat out the order, and he was fingering his revolver so menacingly that I shivered, and the searchers gazed astonished, then slid hastily to the roadway. One came round quite apologetically.

"We were only looking to see if you had any spare grub, Kamerad. Food is none too plentiful for us poor devils," he explained whimsically, offering "Silent Willy" and myself a packet of cigarettes.

"Well, Kamerad, I'm sorry to hear that you're hungry, but my stomach is none too full either," grunted "Silent Willy," and with a flick of his whip started up the horses and left the marines staring down the road after our noisy departure.

It was daylight when we reached the farmhouse, which was old and oak-beamed, set in a walled garden bright with flowers. My uncle and his two sons were just coming from the rose-covered porch to start on the day's work. They stared in wide-eyed amazement when they realized who I was, and seemed struck dumb with my rashness. My uncle took my arm and led me into the kitchen, muttering to himself: "She'll be killed sure as pigs are pigs," and shaking his head dismally.

We sat down to a huge meal of eggs, bacon, new bread and coffee of a quality which we hardly even dreamed about in Roulers now. My soldier companion attacked the meal with silent delight, and eventually rose with a look of beaming happiness so unusual that it quite surprised me. He announced his intention of grooming his horses, which had been put in the stables to rest, after which he proposed to go to sleep in the hay. The horses would be well rested and we could start back whenever I was ready, he reminded me. I told him I wanted to spend the day with my uncle, and that I had thought we might leave at about eleven o'clock that night. I had the rest of the day before me to find out all I could.

The first thing to be done was to get all the information I could from my uncle and his two sons. Three-quarters of an hour later, without stepping over my uncle's doorstep, I had detailed information concerning everything of importance within the area; far more than I had hoped to get; and as regards the second part of my mission (the terminating point of the hidden telephone line), I had some well-grounded clues about that, which should be investigated later. Here, in a nutshell, is what I learned.

My uncle, as a farmer, had to assign a certain amount of his produce to the military authorities. This was taken each week by cart to a large depôt outside Brugge. Sometimes carters were ordered to carry their goods on down to the waterside. Within two kilometres of the docks here was forbidden ground to all but authorized persons. The reason for the brutal severity practised throughout the district lay in the docks. There was a large submarine assembly dock situated there. My cousin was even able to draw a fair plan of it as he had been there several times with his cart.

I also learned that the Marine Corps had recently been heavily reinforced both with guns and men. Large convoys of pontoon bridging material were blocking up the railway approaches to Brugge, and heavy naval guns were beginning to rear their ugly muzzles defiantly in clearings hastily hacked among the beautiful woods by down-at-heel, half-starved Russian prisoners, who had previously been forced to drag them over the dusty, uneven roads.

My uncle also told me that three miles away, by a little clearing beside a grass-covered ride which traversed the woods from our direction, there was a wooden cabin which looked as though it had been wedged between the two tall trees at each side of it. The wood of the hut showed the German War Dept. official stamp. It had stood there since the previous year, and two soldiers lived there. He did not know what the hut was for, it seemed pointless to send two soldiers to live by themselves in the heart of a forest with nothing to guard, but he did know that that hut held the reputation of having always had someone inside it since it was first built. Civilians of Belgian extraction were not encouraged in the neighbourhood of the hut by the two "knubs," but people sometimes passed in the glade going about their business. The hut had become, in fact, one of the stock local mysteries, although through familiarity nobody bothered their heads much about it nowadays. The two "knub" guardians had been nicknamed "The Weather Prophets" by people who lived along the way into Ruddervoorde, because one, known as the Old Woman because of his facial lineaments, seemed always to take his outings when the sun shone, while the other, called the Old Man, for his chubby prematurely wrinkled visage, would generally be seen making his way into Ruddervoorde when the skies were darkening for rain.

During the morning I rested, but although the trials of last night had tired me, I could only doze fitfully. I was impatient and restless to be up and doing. I lay staring at the ceiling and thinking. I wanted to pay a visit to that lonely hut among the trees. What my uncle had told me about the hut and its guardians certainly sounded interesting, but it might very probably not be the place I was looking for. And even if it was, what could I do? For a woman, disguised as a man, to venture out into woods where there were many German working parties which might be met at any moment, was to take a fearful risk of detection. My fair skin, and my hair piled as flatly as possible on top of my head, but nevertheless bulging out my round forage cap, would give me away on near scrutiny. One item stood in my favour. Since the sunshine of the early morning, leaden clouds had rolled across the sky, and swift showers of rain pattered outside. This would give me an excuse to wear my great-coat, whose looseness would hide any tell-tale feminine roundness in my form. When I had thought to myself that far, I knew that in my innermost heart I had decided to go and investigate whatever befell.

After a gigantic midday meal "Silent Willy" returned to his hay bed to sleep it off, and I joined my uncle who was working alone in the garden.

"Uncle Jules," I said, "I am going to take a look at that hut up in the woods."

"You will be taking a terrible risk, Martha; are you not content with what you have learnt already?—But you appear to have no nerves."

"Have you any medical bandages, Uncle Jules, and perhaps an eye-shield suitable for someone who has a weak eye?"

"What do you mean to do, Martha?"

"There must be several hospitals around this district. This afternoon a convalescent soldier is going for a walk in the woods. With my head and chin swathed in a turban of bandages. and an eye-shade over one eye, I don't believe anybody will suspect me of being a woman."

Uncle Jules swore an oath. "I'm not sure that you're not mad, Martha," he chuckled. "Well, we can supply you with the necessary disguise, but your blood be upon your own head, for it is the devil of a risk, and your mother shall not blame me for putting you up to this."

"There is your voice to be considered," warned my uncle. "It is more than possible that some passing soldier may speak to you."

"I have thought of that, too.—A soldier who has been badly wounded about the head and face, and suffered injury to an eye might well have had his tongue injured also. I shall be a dumb soldier, dear uncle."

Three quarters of an hour later a wounded soldier, supporting himself on a stick, slipped through a gap in the hedge at the end of the garden, and having gazed round anxiously to see that his place of origin was unobserved set out into the wet woods, fragrant with the scent of rain-washed herbage.

I soon struck the grass-covered ride which they had told me would lead me to the mysterious hut. I had no idea what I should do when I reached it. I would leave circumstances to decide. I had been walking about half an hour when I heard the hum of voices, and saw that I was coming out into a clearing. I took the battered pipe which Uncle Jules had lent me out of my pocket, and thrusting it between my lips, trudged grimly on with my stick. Russian prisoners were constructing a great gun emplacement beside my path. Two bored sentries smoked leaning on their rifles within five yards of me.

The "knubs" regarded me curiously.

"Hullo, Kamerad, where have you sprung from?" greeted one of them. I winked my one good eye, shook my head and pointed toward my bandaged cheeks. They nodded sympathetically.

"Well—never say die, lad; it was kind of them not to blow your head right off, anyhow," offered the older soldier of the two with a gruff laugh.

The other said: "Your pipe has gone out, Kamerad, take a fill from me." Nodding my thanks I took the proffered pouch and tried to stuff the weed into my bowl with a steady hand. I knew that for the novice in pipe-smoking the difficulty is to pack the pipe in such a way that it will light, but momentarily I could not for the life of me think whether to pack it tightly or loosely, and to bungle the business would look bad. It was an anxious moment as I applied the flame to the tobacco, but to my great relief it lit, and with a farewell wink I continued down the glade and out of sight, puffing clouds of smoke as I went.

I had been walking just over an hour when I sighted the wooden cabin between the two tall trees. Smoke was issuing from the chimney. No human being was in sight. When I had come to within about a hundred yards of it I drew in among the trees beside the glade, watching and pondering as to what I should do. Presently the door opened and a stout soldier came out and strode off down a ride which sloped through the trees in the direction of Ruddervoorde. I wondered whether the soldier who had left the hut was the "Old Man" or the "Old Woman"—judging by the weather it ought to have been the "Old Man." At all events, it meant that there was only one man left in the hut. I felt quite calm now.

A little soldier awoke from his reverie and sat bolt upright in his chair with surprise as I walked in through the open door. Bright blue eyes looked out of a chubby, withered face. Evidently the "Old Man" was at home, and for once the "Weather Prophets" had not played up to their reputation. Perhaps it was as well for me they had not, for this little man must be far less strong physically than the burly "Old Woman."

—"And who the devil may you be?" blurted the "Old Man," looking at me with more curiosity than suspicion. I pointed to my tongue, shaking my head, and he nodded and looked sympathetic as the others had done.

I approached, raised my visible eyebrow and showed him my empty pipe-bowl, then shrugged my shoulders and shook my head with a wink. A minute later we were sitting smoking together, and a kettle was sitting on the iron stove to provide boiling water for my tea. Without speaking a word on my part, we were soon firm friends. Having ascertained that my hearing was still intact, the little man talked to me in his normal voice, and I wrote my replies in pencil on a message-pad which he had handed me. The walls of the cabin were decorated more profusely than artistically with magazine pictures of scantily clad ladies or boxers. But most important of all was the object which sat upon the table. Ringed about with a circle of unwashed crockery was a field telephone.

When the "Old Man" came back from the stove with two steaming cups of tea, I wrote on my message-pad: "What are you doing marooned in the forest in this lonely hut?"

A sly grin spread over his face when he read my question, and he glanced at the field telephone and then winked.

"Aha—that is a secret, Kamarad. Hans and I are very valuable men, you know. We are in charge of something very special up here.—But we don't invite inquisitive Kamarads to come and visit us."

"You are lucky," I wrote. "This is a pretty 'cushy' job compared to sharing one's meals with the rats in the trenches."

"You are certainly right there," he agreed. "Hans and I know all about life in the trenches. We've had our bellyful of that, to be sure. Then one day a message came up: 'Two steady experienced signallers wanted. Must be highly intelligent, sober, of quiet habits and thoroughly discreet and trustworthy when not under supervision.'—Well, it didn't take them two minutes to hit on Hans and me.—They knew we were not just scatter-brained fools like the young fellows, never knowing how to do anything unless they were shouted at.—'You are one of my best men,' says the Herr Hauptmann," mused the "Old Man," pouring his tea into his saucer and gulping it down. "Always used to send for me when he had anything special to be done.—Yes, he knew his job did the Herr Hauptmann."

"You make me feel very interested about this important job the authorities have entrusted you with," I scribbled, and I saw the little man puff himself as he read it.

"I'll bet you can never guess who's at the other end of that telephone," he whispered mysteriously.

"Somebody pretty high up on the Staff, eh?" questioned my note.

"Huh, Staff!" he chortled to himself. I'm employed on something more important than talking to staff officers.—The man at the other end of that line," he pronounced in an impressive undertone, "is a so-called priest behind the enemy lines."

I tried to register amazement and admiration with my visible eye.

"Does he send you through much information?" I passed across to him.

"I should think so. Every day we hear from him," he assured me. "Yes, by God, if the British knew all that Hans and I get to know about them, they'd be after our blood right enough!"

"I suppose one of you two has always to be in the hut in case he rings through," I wrote.

"That's so," he nodded. "He usually speaks as the dusk is coming on; but he may, of course, put through an emergency call at any time. However, Hans and I are steady men. We like our mug of beer and our pipe down with the Kamarads in Ruddervoorde now and then, but we don't mind taking our turn up here alone."

I glanced at the battered watch which dangled by its chain from a nail. It was nearly five o'clock. Dusk would fall about eight o'clock, and I did not feel it would be prudent to remain in the hut much longer. Besides, the "Old Woman" might return to complicate matters, nor had I decided then what I was going to do and I wanted to be alone to think. My next note informed my host that it was time for me to be getting back to the hospital, thanked him for his hospitality, and said that I hoped to pay him another visit before long.

Then I rose, leaning heavily on my stick, and nodded to the "Old Man," who invited me breezily to look in at the hut whenever I felt so inclined. As an afterthought I bent over the table and composed my last message: "I suppose there is no chance of Hans coming back to relieve you, and you being able to walk down with me into Ruddervoorde for a glass together?"

"Thanks, Kamarad," he replied, "not this time, I'm afraid. Hans won't be back till nine or later, this evening."

So the "Old Man" would be alone at dusk when the telephone-bell would hum, telling that somewhere behind the British lines some shabbily cassocked village *curé* was crouched listening anxiously for a guttural greeting. I had taken the ride which led down towards Ruddervoorde, but as soon as the cabin was out of sight, I slipped in among the trees and made my way back until within about a hundred yards of the hut, where I sat down, sheltered by the lightning-split bole of a great tree. I intended to remain there until the dusk was about to fall, and then to reconnoitre closer about the hut, and perhaps creep within ear shot of the open window. It was a warm evening and as the window had been open when I left, I hoped he would keep it so. As I sat there in the gloom of the forest listening to the murmuring whisper of the rain among the branches and the steady drip of water from above, I was thinking of the little chloroform bottle which was in my great-coat pocket and whether I might not overpower the "Old Man," for I was certainly bigger than he was—and by that means myself get in communication with the spy. It seemed a wild scheme and for long I turned it over in my mind without making any definite decision.

The hours of waiting seemed interminable, and I had fallen into a reverie in which my mind hardly functioned at all, when I suddenly woke up to the fact that the leaden sky had grown darker and the atmosphere itself seemed to have grown dim amid a strange stillness. It was twilight. Pulling my wrist-watch from my tunic pocket, for it was gold and dainty, hardly suitable to the wrist of a "knub," I found it was eight o'clock. I soaked the pad I had brought in chloroform, replaced it in my pocket, then jumped to my feet and walked boldly towards the cabin. The wet turf muffled my footsteps and as I passed the window I saw the "Old Man" sitting with his stockinged feet propped on a corner of the table as he read and smoked his curly pipe by the light of two flickering candles. I rapped loudly on the door with my stick. There was a pause, the creak of a chair, then footsteps and the "Old Man" was peering curiously at me round the door.

"Well, I'll be damned!" he ejaculated, pulling the door wide. "You again, Kamarad—and where have you sprung from?"

I gestured vaguely towards the trees, shrugged my shoulders and shook my head, trying to imply that I had lost my way.

"Well, well—come in and write it down," he advised, and turned to take the message-pad and pencil from the table.

My stick was rough-cut with a thick and heavy knob at the end. The moment he turned I whirled it and struck him sharply on the back of the head. He staggered, dazed, and I rushed at him and clasped the chloroform-pad tightly over his face. For a moment or two, the little man swayed drunkenly, waving his arms like a drowning swimmer then he crumpled limply backwards. I tore a blanket off one of the beds and ripping it into strips with a table-knife bound him hand and foot, for there was always the risk that he might recover from the chloroform fumes before I was ready. The light breeze from the windows brushed the candle flames and the dim cabin was full of dancing light and shadows. Only the long-drawn breathing of the unconscious man disturbed the stillness of the forest. I sat down trying to be calm and watched the telephone eagerly. That bell might begin to hum at any moment now. Perhaps it might not hum at all.

I gazed at the watch hanging on the wall and watched the minutes go by. A quarter of an hour—half an hour—as I sat fingering the chair-rests nervously. Still the heavy breathing behind me came regularly. I did not know when my victim would wake up and start struggling to free himself. Then there was the fat Hans. I did not know at what minute he might walk in at the door. I began to wring damp hands, praying that that ghastly silent brown leather case would burst into humming life before it was too late. Somehow I felt within me that inevitably the case would speak that night, but would it speak in time?—Restlessness drove me from my chair to pacing the cabin. I found myself listening for noises in the forest.—The brown case had started to hum persistently.—I seized the receiver with shaking hands, hardly able to believe my senses.

My voice was contralto and I spoke as low and evenly as possible to simulate a man speaking.

"Well—what's your news?" I said. I felt a quiver of nervous emotion in my throat but forced myself to speak naturally.

"Who are you? Your voice is strange," came to me in German from the other end, and in what sounded like the voice of an old man.

"I am new here. This is an officer speaking," I sent back. "I have serious news for you, but all will be well if you carry out our instructions. First of all, let me have your report."—I did not trouble to note the information he read over the phone, it was of no use to me and I had only asked him for it to gain his confidence.

"Now, listen," I ordered when he had finished. "Early this morning a British aeroplane appeared out of the dawn. It was thought that it was making for Zeebrugge, but when it came over the telephone-hut in the woods, it suddenly dived and loosed a number of incendiary bombs upon the hut and the surrounding trees."—There was a sound behind me. The bound form on the floor behind me was heaving, tossing and grunting vehemently, seeming to heave itself about the floor in a series of jumps. I glanced round fearfully, praying the knots would hold. The eyes were glaring like those of a savage animal in my direction, and the body was edging nearer.

"What happened after that?" the distant voice was inquiring in my ear.

"The trees caught alight, and a great fire started. The hut and much of the telephone line for some distance were completely destroyed. The two operators were killed. We tapped into the line at the point where it still remained intact, and that is where I am talking from now——"

"Then the British must have known of the existence of the line, or they would not have attacked the hut," broke in the voice, and there was fear in it.

"They must have got information from somewhere," I agreed. "We thought that you might have been captured. It is certain that for some days to come it will be dangerous for you to visit your end of the line. You are too valuable to lose, you must keep away. If they have not done so already, the British will almost certainly be keeping a very vigilant look out."

"Thank God for this warning," muttered the man in the distance.

"We have not yet decided what our procedure for gaining information is to be under these new circumstances. But in four days' time an aeroplane will drop a man by parachute behind the British lines who will give you your instructions. This will take place soon after dawn on the 15th.—You have your map with you?" I guessed that he would have one, for in the information he had given me he had mentioned several references on a gridded map of the fighting area.—"Very well," I continued, when he replied in the affirmative. "Give the map reference of some deserted spot well behind the line where the agent can be safely landed. You will meet him there."

I carefully noted down the reference he gave me after a short pause.

"Good-bye, and good luck," I said and replaced the receiver. The little man had wriggled himself to my feet now, but he lay there exhausted, amazement and hatred fought in his eyes. Thank God the knots had held, or I think either one or other of us would have been dead within a few minutes. I was sorry for the "Old Man," for he was a good fellow.

With a gasp of relief I ran from the hut. It was fine now and the air was fresh, with the moon sailing among the clouds.

Pale moonlight made the tree-tops silvery and lit the glades. Walking slowly towards the hut was a dark figure, perhaps fifty yards away. Hans was come home. He stopped dead when he saw my body silhouetted in the light of the doorway, then he gave a hoarse shout and began running towards the hut.

I turned and fled to the darkness behind the hut, and then in among trees and undergrowth, crashing and tripping, gasping with terror, running as I had never run before. When I paused to listen I could hear nobody following. Perhaps he had been too astonished at first. Wet with perspiration I made my way slowly back towards the vicinity of the ride which had led me from the farm-house. It was a quarter past ten when I crept back through the back garden, tore the bandages off my head and peered in cautiously through the kitchen window. My uncle, who was seated by the fire, hurried to the door when I tapped I on the glass.

"I was waiting for you, Martha," he exclaimed. "Everything has gone well, eh?— Thank God you are returned, at least."

"Everything has gone well," I assured him. "But I think the less that you know about it the better for the family." My uncle nodded.

"The soldier who brought you here wanted to know at supper where you had gone," he said. "We told him that you had gone to see neighbours. He was greatly agitated, saying it was most imprudent for you to venture outside in uniform, and swearing that he would get into terrible trouble if your presence was detected, so if he starts chiding you in a minute, do not be taken aback, but start talking about some imaginary neighbours nearby."

I threw my bandage and eye-shade into the fire, and fetching an axe, chopped my thick knobbed stick to pieces, and sent these to follow the other possible clues to my identity. The remains of the chloroform went down the sink, the fragments of the bottle and the pad for purification into the flames.

At one o'clock in the morning, an empty wagon, the property of the 52nd M.-G. Company, with two silent "knubs" jolting on the box-seat, was rumbling back towards Roulers. My uncle had presented "Silent Willy" with two bottles of *Schnapps* and a bulky package of fresh sausages before we left the farm. The soldier's eyes had gleamed with gratitude—"*Schnapps* and sausages—*Schnapps* and sausages. It was worth it, mein Gott!" he had muttered to himself as we started, afterwards lapsing into his usual mood of reflection. That night's work was also worth a firing-party to him, but fortunately for his peace of mind and his appetite, he will never know that unless he reads this!

I felt happy and satisfied. I knew my information about Brugge was of great value, and besides, in regard to the rendezvous I had arranged with the spy, the British would be able to establish his identity and shadow him until he visited his hidden telephone terminal again, while my warning would keep him away from it until it was too late for his friends to inform him of my deception.

I handed my news to No. 63 the following night.

~

The week that followed was a time of anxiety for me. I had heard no word from my uncle. I did not know what had taken place after I had run from the hut. It seemed to me that Otto had become more pleasantly friendly and attentive to me than usual. Perhaps this was the imagination of a guilty conscience, yet it really did seem to me that he sought my society more, and I was frightened.

One morning, one of the dressers approached me as soon as I arrived at the hospital.

"Fräulein, the Oberartz said he wished to see you in the office as soon as you arrived." My knees shook. In the ordinary course of things the Oberartz never interviewed me in this room. I was terrified as I went towards the office, and my head seemed full of a strange buzzing.

With the Oberartz was the Town-Major. My last hope went. The end would probably be a firing-party in the dawn.

"I congratulate you, Fräulein." The Oberartz stood up, shook my hand and beamed on me. I stared dumbly. Was this a joke?

"His Royal Highness the King of Würtemburg has graciously indicated that you have been awarded the Iron Cross for fine work with this hospital."

I nearly fainted with relief, then laughed hysterically. Presently I was sitting in a chair while the Oberartz held a glass to my lips. The same day Canteen Ma brought a message for me in a pin-cushion. It simply said: "Many thanks—the submarine base was news to us"—but from such a quarter, this was praise indeed!

CHAPTER VI

Summer had come. The sun shone down brilliantly on life in Roulers and the songs of the birds made a pleasant contrast to the almost incessant roll of gun-fire. Stray shells still soared over the town occasionally, but they usually exploded in the air or plunged harmlessly into the fields. Curiously enough, for all that year the casualties from shell-fire had only been two aged cart-horses, which were to be sent to the knacker's yard within a few days in any case!

It suddenly began to strike me that something unusual was happening in Roulers. There was a tremendous air of animation among the Germans, but their activity was of a new kind and not like that which used to take place before an attack. Sometimes it looked as though our conquerers had all gone mad. Fatigue parties spent their days polishing the floors of the hospital till they glimmered like glass, and men were tying rags on the end of long poles in order to dust the lofty ceilings. In the streets the German soldiers walked in clean new uniforms, and their equipment seemed to have lost its battered appearance. Squads paraded in the streets, moving like automatons, practising the goose-step with eyes and faces of wood. Alphonse grumbled to me that he had had to spend the whole of the last evening, after returning from a heavy day with the ambulance under fire, in polishing and burnishing an aluminium bath in his barrack-room, and that when he had proudly displayed it glistening like a mirror to the hospital sergeant-major, he had condemned it as terrible and called him an idler. He said that the troops in all the billets throughout Roulers were being put to work in the same way, and that everywhere the officers were making themselves unpleasant to the N.C.O.'s, and that consequently these were working off their resentment twofold on the men. He told me that one old soldier who had been a conscript before the War, said grimly that things were beginning to get quite like the good old times again!

I asked one of the doctors in the hospital what all the excitement was about. He said nobody knew, but that H.Q. had suddenly decided for some reason to hurl the full force of its frightfulness upon the Roulers authorities, and that we were all feeling the concussion. I knew there must be some reason for this. Then one day Alphonse met me in the corridor. He paused for a moment in passing and said in an undertone:

"The Kaiser is due at Menin next week. He will be coming on here later.—Can you find out the date and time?"

So that was it. I might have guessed. All that day I racked my brains how to get reliable information. Suppose that I succeeded in bringing about the death of the German Emperor. It was said that it was he who was responsible for the War; what, therefore, would happen at his death?—A sharp thrill of excitement ran through me, and I determined that there musl be no mistake in this affair. Yet who in Roulers could provide me with the necessary information? It was well known that the Kaiser always kept his movements as secret as possible for fear of attempts on his life. The

Monday of the week before the Kaiser's expected visit came, but my head was empty of ideas and I began to despair.

"Canteen Ma" called at the door early. As she handed me our weekly vegetables and I was examining them for freshness she slipped a pincushion into my hand.—So they also knew! When I ripped open the pincushion in my room the message read:

"Kaiser arrives Roulers latter half next week for brief inspection. Time and Date, etc., for information British aircraft."

Elegant staff-officers with tight waists and important faces began to flood Roulers. Then generals arrived in cars, and everybody went about in a bad temper. The General Staff were arrived in person to see that everything in Roulers was fit for the eyes of the mighty war-lord, and the heel-clicking could have been heard in Ypres.

When I answered a summons to the Oberartz' office on the Tuesday morning in the week before the expected Royal visit, he was seated with a tall Staff Colonel, one of these steely-blue-eyed men with fierce fair moustaches brushed upwards. He rose smartly upon being introduced, bowed, clicked his heels, smiled in a refined manner, and bowed again. The Oberartz asked me to show the Colonel round the wards and to explain everything to him, excusing himself on the count that a number of bad cases had just been brought in and that his presence was needed in the operating theatre.

The Colonel followed me round, always seeming interested, always courteous. He never found fault with anything, and from time to time uttered well-bred little jokes to me which evidently amused him tremendously and which I pretended to be much amused at myself. He was certainly a very polished person. As we approached the door of the Oberartz' office on our return, he surprised me by suddenly saying:

"Perhaps if you find yourself free you would care to lunch with me to-morrow, mein Fräulein?"

The Colonel had shown himself to be a talkative man, and I saw a glimmer of hope in this direction.

"There is nothing would please me better, Herr Colonel," I assured him.

It might be said of that lunch next day that we got along "famously." At the end he swallowed his liqueur and called for a second.

"Mein Fräulein," he smiled, "life must be tedious in the extreme here in Roulers, for a girl of your standing and education." He gestured with his cigarette gracefully. "Would you not care to come for a while to Brussels, to see the opera, to eat decent food?"

I coloured. Food was not what he was thinking about. His hand clasped my wrist.

"Do not be afraid, little one," he soothed. "It shall be as you wish. I shall not urge you. Come—and I will strive my utmost to make your stay a pleasure. I will personally guarantee your safety, and I can procure for you a special pass.—And now I will escort you to the hospital, Fräulein. As for what I suggest, it is for you to decide." He rose and pulled back my chair.

Near the hospital gates the road was deserted and he paused and caught my arm. Then gently raising my chin so that his blue eyes gazed into mine he murmured:

"Well, have you decided, mein Fräulein?"

I had been thinking furiously during the walk to the hospital.

"Herr Colonel," I said, "I have decided. I will stay with you in Brussels."

He kissed my hand gently.

"What excuse will you make to obtain leave of absence from the hospital?" he asked, a trifle anxiously.

"My grandmother lives in Brussels. I will tell the Herr Oberartz that she is very ill and is asking to see me, and that you, Herr Colonel, have had the goodness to procure for me a pass."

"That is so," he laughed, "I am a good Samaritan, indeed!" His arm was about my shoulder, and I think he would have kissed me had not a couple of young officers turned into the street and saluted him rigidly as they passed. "Take the evening train to-morrow," he went on, his eyes returning to mine. "You should be at Brussels soon after midnight. It is possible I may have night work, I do not know. At all events my orderly shall meet you and bring you to my hotel, where a room shall be ready for you. I shall hope for the honour of your presence at breakfast at eight-thirty the following morning."

"I shall not be able to obtain leave for more than four days from the Oberartz," I told him; for I had rapidly calculated that that was the longest I could afford to find out the information I wanted, if I was to return to Roulers and transmit what I knew over the frontier I might hear nothing, but on the other hand this man was on the General Staff, and I might well trick him into speaking in an unguarded moment.

The Colonel saluted.

"Mein Fräulein," he said softly, "it will be four days of Paradise. Until eight-thirty Friday, and the pass shall reach you to-morrow morning."

He bent sharply from the waist, straightened, turned about and swaggered gaily up the dusty road. I stood watching his receding back, and the scent of the clusters of heliotrope on a nearby wall came to me on the warm air. It all seemed unreal and dream-like. Had I really promised this stranger that I would spend four days with him in Brussels? Was I mad? To what had I committed myself? What chance had I of coming through such an escapade unscathed? Why had I done it? For the sake of ravished Belgium. The thought comforted me, and I hurried through the grey stone gates and busied myself with other things.

On the Thursday morning before I left for the hospital a German soldier brought an official envelope to the café. It held the special pass and a travelling voucher. I said nothing to my mother of where I was going; for, although she encouraged me in spying, I was afraid to tell her of the extreme risk to which I had now committed myself. I did warn her, however, that that night I had a long errand to perform which might keep me away for several days, but there was no cause for unusual anxiety. Now that my course was set, I felt no qualms. If I succeeded no sacrifice could be too great. I left a note for "Canteen Ma" giving her all details, and requesting as an afterthought that some other secret agent might be near me in the hotel in case of trouble, or in case I was myself unable to transmit information I was able to obtain. I suggested that an agent might pick me up at my hotel in Brussels by reason of the fact that always, when not in evening dress, I would wear a buttonhole of mixed snowdrops and violets without any green leaves at my collar.

A German military car was waiting outside the darkened station at Brussels, and the driver had soon settled me comfortably inside with my single suitcase. He handed me a note from the Colonel, excusing himself for his enforced absence and assuring me that for the future he had made arrangements that he should not be so detained.

~

I awoke next morning to find a trim maid letting up the blinds and flooding my spacious, unfamiliar bedroom with dazzling sunbeams. The silken curtains, the rich pile carpets, the wallpaper, and the soft billowing eiderdown were of deep peacock blue, and the dark furniture and the electric stove gleamed brightly. Upon the tray on which was my morning coffee was a small note in the Colonel's handwriting, and I did not need to open it to find a dead weight clutching at my heart. It had brought me back to realities. Within the hour I must meet my Colonel, and then what would follow? But somewhere near here was the Kaiser!—How I hated this man whom I had never seen. This man whose vandals had overrun my country. I must keep a clear head no matter what should happen. And, ruminating thus, I dressed.

My Colonel was delighted when I appeared in the spacious dining-room, and he devoured a huge breakfast with a light heart and much excited chatter. Being Belgian, and quite un-used to a heavy meal and so much good-humour at this early hour, I felt somewhat overwhelmed. After I had seen him off with promises to meet at lunch, I determined on a visit to the shops.

Walking along the Rue Royale towards the Grand Place it was heart-rending to see the change in beautiful "Petite Paris." Captured Allied guns stood in every possible space, some placarded with inspired news. The roadways badly needed repairs. It all looked shabby in the extreme. The thought struck me that I would like to let loose an army of mad painters to work their will no matter what the result, so long as that drab, seedy look was eliminated. It suddenly

struck me too that, irony of ironies! it was the 21st of July!—
Belgium's Independence Day, and here were a horde of
marauders in field-grey lording it in Beautiful Brussels. The
passers-by did not seem cowed by any manner of means.
Thank God, every one wore a stiff upper lip.

The shops were a great disappointment. "It is regrettable,
Mademoiselle, but we are unable to renew anything. Our stock
is being gradually decreased, and where we are going to get fresh
stock from, only the good Lord can say." The prices asked took
my breath away. The half-blue painted shop-windows wore a
thin look, for dummy show was everywhere. I nearly wept.
I thought I would take a look at the old Grand Place. It was
a spot that had always a restful appeal to me. Its noble and
towering architecture would drive away my fit of blues.

Turning into the Boulevard Anspach I saw, trudging
along, a company of English soldiers. Their prisoners'
uniforms were dreadfully shabby, patches everywhere, and
with pitiful, down-at-heel boots. The company drew along
the kerb as a tramway-car clanged its way down the street.
As the car drew level with the prisoners a shower of cigarettes
and tablets of chocolate fell amongst them from the windows.
One of the German guards caught sight of the person on
the tramcar who had thrown the edibles. With a loud shout
he mounted the moving tram to arrest the culprit who had
dared to violate a strict order. The civilian, seeing that he was
discovered, vaulted lightly over the iron gate of the tramcar
and made rapidly for a side-street off the Boulevard Anspatch,
the soldier following in hot pursuit, his rifle held at the
ready. As the soldier arrived at the opposite footpath, he was
obstructed by a small crowd of civilians who in their haste to
get out of his way encumbered him the more. Suddenly I saw
a foot slyly pushed forward, and the soldier lay sprawled and

cursing on the footpath. The foot belonged to the mysterious safety-pin man whom I had last seen that night in the café, when he had stabbed the military policeman and effected the double escape. He faded into the crowd.

The Colonel had returned, and we had just sat down to lunch when I was aware of the noise of distant cheers, which gradually swelled closer, till I could distinguish that they came from Belgian throats; the tramcars passing the hotel seemed to clang their bells with a louder, more insistent warning, and the commotion outside grew in volume. Springing to our feet we hurried into the entrance lobby. The door was packed with the guests all straining their necks upwards. I gradually pushed my way through, and there a sight met my eyes which thrilled me through and through. An enormous toy balloon was floating free and unfettered 250 feet above us. It was bedecked in Belgium's national colours, the envelope painted with the Tricolour of France and Union Jack of Britain. Long streamers flew proudly from the sides. "Vive la Belgique," "Vive les Alliés," embossed thereon. It sailed majestically along in the faint July breeze. A defiant gesture, and a reminder to the invader that Belgium was still, in soul, free and independent.

It was amazing to see the electrical effect on the civilians. Laughing jokes and words of encouragement were passed to each other as they went by, heads were held more erect. The Belgian tram-car drivers beat a methodical and persistent tattoo on the tram-bells, motor-drivers gave answering toots, the cabbies cracked their whips defiantly. Deafening noises of all descriptions rent the air until a muttering roar rose over the whole city as the emblem of freedom slowly swept away. I heard the sharp crack, crack, of rifles. The military authorities had given orders for the offending emblem to be destroyed.

At each crack the tumult swelled the louder, until a final crack and the envelope was no more. The muttering roar grew fainter and fainter, but Brussels had celebrated its Independence Day!

The Colonel was furious over the affair.

"Himmel," he said, "the organizers of such an outrage, a few irresponsible youths I suppose, little think what the result of such a stupid escapade can mean for the town."

"After all," I reminded him innocently, "we have to celebrate our Independence Day some way or another. And then our Independence is only eighty-five years of age!—Youth will have its fling, you know."

In the evening my gallant entertainer conducted me to a motor-car. No orders were given, the driver evidently knew his destination. During our short journey I noticed that all the street-lamps and tram-car lights were painted a dark blue. The sky was slashed by the long beams of questing searchlights, and the distant staccato of anti-aircraft guns told of the activity of Allied raiders. The car pulled up at the entrance to an imposing private residence, set in its own grounds amid trees and shrubs. Several motor-cars were parked in the grounds. A ring at the door-bell, a muttered conversation, and we were allowed to enter.

Strains of soft dance music greeted us as I let the attendant take my cloak. We descended marble steps into a beautifully appointed room, profusely decked with flowers and fragrant with perfume. Along one side of the room were red-curtained alcoves, and windows opened on to a shadowy lawn along the other side. Ranged round a small dance-floor in the centre were tables. At these tables I saw noisy parties of officers of all services, and with them sat many beautiful girls with tired eyes, some Belgian, some German. Most of them were voluptuously wanton in their behaviour, for the champagne was flowing freely.

A bowing waiter led us to an alcove, and champagne was served to us. The hidden orchestra broke into a lively dance-tune. Almost without exception the officers wore that German class mark, a horrid gash down the side of the face received in some fencing brawl. Some wore monocles, and all had closely cropped hair. And the women—but who am I to judge, for my own countrywomen were there too! If asked, every one of them would have a harrowing tale to tell. Hounded down, driven to distraction by punishments meted out to their kinsfolk, subject to atrocities and unmentionable acts of outrage, they were caught in a holocaust over which they had no control, until they were literally driven into the arms of their oppressors by sheer want and starvation, utterly bewildered by a world gone mad. In all conscience the blame lay at the door of the invaders. The place was an ultra-select night rendezvous, a product and importation of warring Germany.

As the night passed into morning, the company became madly uproarious, singing in uncertain chorus, shouting and embracing. Three noisy late-comers, very drunk, were going the rounds of the centre tables. One of them, a Lutheran minister, carrying a huge stock-whip, beat a drunken tattoo on each table with the whip, until, at one table, unable to keep his balance, he swept off several glasses which fell to the ground with a shattering noise. Wine stained one of the girl's dresses. She struck the minister savagely in the face. He raised his whip, calling her "A filthy Belgian sow." The other officers at the table grew excited.—He was pushed away and fell crashing on to another table with a roar of rage.

The scene might have developed into a very nasty episode, for I saw the Colonel's face grow set, but for a stern interruption from the entrance.

"Gentlemen," grated a harsh voice, "by orders of the General Commanding, all officers must report to units at once. All civilians not of German nationality must produce their identity cards for my inspection."

Faint screams of protest came from the frightened girls who hurried out of the room to seek for identity cards. The Colonel gripped my arm and whispered:

"Say nothing. I will arrange this with the feld-major. Von Bissing has lost no time. His chastisement of the town for the balloon imprudence comes quickly."

When we reached the hotel we heard that Brussels was to be fined 8,000,000 marks, and that curfew was to be curtailed to five o'clock until further notice.

Three days passed at the hotel while the Colonel entertained me in the intervals of arduous duty. Had he not been an enemy officer he would have seemed a very pleasant companion. He was courteous, and honestly tried to do all he could to please me. I knew that I greatly attracted him, but beyond caressing my arm or my hand, and presenting me with flowers and small presents, he had paid me none of the attentions I had expected from his manner in Roulers.

Nor had he once visited my room.

Then on the next morning, I returned to my room in the hotel after I had been shopping, to see the door standing half-open. At first I thought it was the servant who was late in cleaning out the room, but when I pushed the door wide, a German soldier was standing with his back to me gazing out of the open window. He had just placed two strange suitcases on the ground beside the bed. Then he touched his military cap, and smirking faintly walked out without a word.

I knew what this meant. There could be no mistake in the rooms, for the Colonel's initials were on the suitcases. I sat down upon the edge of the bed, aghast. In my silly optimism I had begun to think I might learn what I wanted without having to go to such an extreme. I felt horribly lonely and frightened in a world of savage ogres as I dug my fingers miserably into the silk eiderdown, and the tears welled to my eyes.

But this was absurd. Anything which had come to pass I had brought upon myself. I was a Secret Service agent, not a ridiculous young girl. I looked at my wrist-watch, and it was about the hour when the Colonel returned to the hotel from his morning's work. He would probably be waiting for me over his vermouth in the lounge at this moment. Perhaps smiling to himself at the trick he had played me. But was it a trick? Could I have expected anything else? I left the bed, powdered my nose, tidied my hair, and slowly proceeded downstairs wondering how the Colonel would greet me.

In the lounge the Colonel left the palm-shaded alcove where he had been sitting and approached me with his well-bred smile. Bowing, he kissed my hand and conducted me back to his alcove, after ordering further drinks. He was suave and his talk was of trivialities. He made not the slightest hint about the suitcases in my bedroom. For the first time since I had arrived in Brussels I began to worry seriously as to where was that other agent whom I had requested should if possible keep me secret company. I had received no sign and had no idea where to look. So far I had got nothing out of my Colonel, and while he talked I was thinking to myself that I wanted the company of a friend very much.

As my eye wandered round the busy lounge an announcement of a Command Concert at the Opera House for that night, suspended from a pillar, caught my attention. I asked the Colonel to take me.

"Certainly, mein Fraulein," he smiled. "It is a good suggestion." Then he stroked up his moustache and gazed naively at the ceiling. "Music will be a fitting prelude to other delights," he continued. "Incidentally, to-night at the Opera is a great gala night, for the All Highest will be present."

My heart leaped. I determined that we should dine well that night, so well that wine should unlock his tongue. It did, but not to the extent that I had wanted. At the Opera there was a dense crowd of military men but few civilians. When the All Highest entered and the orchestra crashed out "Deutschland Uber Alles," all leaped to their feet like one great wave. Then followed prolonged cheering while the audience remained standing. I thought there sounded a note of artificiality in those cheers. The Kaiser took scant notice of the people all around him. As he listlessly sat back in his box among his glittering staff I detected a sad look on his face, as though bowed down by the weight of responsibility. And here was I, a spy, within a few yards of him, planning his death! The Colonel pressed my hand in the darkness of the box and I felt his lips brush my neck.

"Why do you look nowhere but at the All Highest, with that strange look in your eyes, my angel? Come, will you not pay a little attention to me?" he whispered, and it seemed to me that I started as though struck, but apparently he noticed nothing.

Back once more in the hotel we drank coffee and brandy in the lounge. My host leaned across the table. As he lit a match for his cigar his hand trembled. His breath smelt of alcohol, which was unusual for him. I looked away, not daring to think, and the disappointment of having been able to make him disclose nothing made it all seem so painfully futile. Soon now I should be alone with him and—a German lieutenant at the next table but one deliberately winked at me and looked away. For a moment I did not understand. The Colonel was talking but I heard nothing. Was this perhaps my secret agent? Within a minute or two the lieutenant looked at me again, nodded faintly, got to his feet and walked to the lift.

"Come, little one," suggested the Colonel, rising a trifle unsteadily; "you are perhaps tired. We will go to our room."

Upstairs he took me in his arms.

"In a little while I shall return," he told me, looking toward my nightdress which was laid out on the peacock-blue eiderdown, and he went out with a smile, gently closing the door behind him. I stared round the room, not knowing what to do next. Then I approached the window, let up the blind and gazed out on the calm night. Below in the depths ran a side-street, for my room was at the side of the hotel, and beyond stretched the roof-tops and spires of Brussels, rising so silent, gaunt, unsympathetic in the moonlight.

A light balcony lay outside my window and, opening it, I stepped through. The soft night wind ruffled my hair and seemed to give confidence to my burning senses. Suddenly a figure appeared upon the balcony next to mine. It was a man, and he made a warning gesture with his hand. Only a few yards separated us. He slipped over the narrow space, gripped my rail, and in a moment we were standing peering into each other's faces.

I caught his hand and drew him into the light of the bedroom. It was the German lieutenant who had winked at me in the lounge, except that now he was clad in a black and scarlet brocaded dressing-gown beneath which I caught a glimpse of blue silk pyjamas. He grinned and smoothed crisp tousled hair. Then he lifted the lapel of his dressing-gown, showed me two diagonally placed safety-pins nestling there, and laughed.

"Good evening," he murmured. "I am an Englishman. I am on the Secret Intelligence in Brussels. There are several of us here. I daresay you were surprised to see me in a German uniform, but personally I was fitted into this job by our War Office before the War got started. We received warning of the important job you were on, and I was detailed to shadow you."

"You recognized the violets and snowdrops without leaves?"

"Yes," he nodded, and then took out his cigarette-case, opened it, but suddenly, as an afterthought, shut it again sadly. "S'pose I'd better not smoke," he decided. "Old Colonel might smell it when he came back. Look here, have you succeeded in getting anything out of him? Tell me, what can I do to assist?"

"So far I have been unable to learn anything, but perhaps I shall know something before to-morrow morning." There was silence between us. "To-night is going to be rather a difficult one for me," I explained a little ruefully.

He nodded, looking grave.

"I wish I could help you," he said.

"You couldn't," I assured him. "It would only throw suspicion on both of us if you try to help me actively. I must rely on myself to-night. But here is where you can help. Suppose that I do manage to ascertain the information I want within time to make use of it, I intend to get back to Roulers immediately, as I can transmit the warning quicker direct over the frontier and thence by the regular channel to the Air authorities near the line than you would be able to do from here."

"You may throw suspicion upon yourself by trying to run away," he put in.

"I don't think so" I replied. "Why should he suspect me, and what could he prove even if he did? The line I shall take from now onwards is the frightened and virtuous young girl, and that would be my excuse for running away. In any case, I believe he would be somewhat anxious to keep my disappearance quiet from his friends, especially as he had no right to give me a special pass to Brussels in the first place.—However," I continued, "it is possible that I shall not be able to elude the Colonel. In that case, as a warning to you of this fact, I shall wear green leaves with the bunch of snowdrops and violets at my collar, and I shall place my message in the ring of the steel bracket which clamps the water-pipe to the wall between our two balconies."

"I understand," he rejoined, and then looked hard at the Colonel's two suitcases which still stood untouched where the soldier had placed them by the bed. "Do those cases belong to your precious Colonel?" he inquired.

"Yes."

"Have you searched them for papers?"

"Not yet."

He was down on his knees in a moment.

"Fortunately they are unlocked," he muttered, hastily running his hand through the contents with the hand of an expert, so that he did not disturb them. He drew out a packet of papers and ran through them with swift eagerness. He selected three and pushed the rest back whence they came.

"Nothing of much value," he grinned, removing one scarlet slipper and stuffing them inside. "But better than nothing, all the same."

He had one leg poised in the air as he replaced the slipper, when there sounded a rap on the door.

"The Colonel," I gasped.

Then the door-handle began to turn. I choked back a scream. Turning I saw—nothing. The Lieutenant had vanished. But he could not possibly have escaped through the window in time. There were no cupboards for a man of his size. He had taken refuge beneath the bed.

The Colonel smiled a trifle vacantly, and then encircled me in his arms.

"You have not yet undressed, my angel," he chided. "Ah, but I see that you were about to unpack my cases," he said, his gaze falling upon the two open suitcases which the Lieutenant had abandoned. His lips sought mine, while my mind was in a whirl. What could I do? I must play for time. Somehow I must give the Lieutenant a chance to slip over the balcony into his own room.

"I cannot stay here after to-night," I whispered. "I am frightened—besides, what will the Herr Oberartz say at the hospital if I am absent when the All Highest arrives? There are various duties in the hospital which are specially assigned to me and it is essential that I should be present."

"Do not worry," replied the Colonel, "we have two days yet, and your leave can be extended. He arrives on Saturday to review the troops at eleven o'clock, and will afterwards inspect the place. He will not even stay the night, so that he will only take a cursory glance all round. I think that you could perfectly well stay away for the All Highest's visit altogether. What do you say, my sweet?"

So, at least I knew what I had set out to learn!

"I promised the Oberartz I would return," I mumbled, hardly aware of what I was saying, for I was thinking feverishly of the man under my bed and what would happen if he were found. My lover held me close and pressed his lips on mine. I did not care, I was thinking, thinking furiously, desperately. In another room down the corridor German voices were singing. Sing—how could anybody in the world sing when such a ghastly dilemma was playing itself out in this bedroom?

Somebody was walking along the passage. Little did they think of what was being enacted in here. Suddenly there came a tremendous crash of glass, and then oaths followed by peals of unsteady laughter. The Colonel relaxed his hold, listening. In a second I was at the door, for whatever it might be it offered some momentary respite. Outside, a blear-eyed Saxon officer of middle age swayed gently to and fro in an ecstasy of delight, and aimlessly brandished an empty wine-glass, in admonition of a silent waiter who was collecting heaps of shattered glass upon his tray. Crowded in a nearby doorway and peeping over each other's shoulders were the Saxon's comrades, applauding loudly. I hoped the Colonel would follow me out of the room, and so I rushed up to the gallant Saxon and asked what was the matter.

The officer stiffened and made an attempt at a bow which nearly overbalanced him, and then said:

"Believe me, the explanation is quite simple Fräulein. This pig-dog and myself tried to pass in the passage, but as you see there was not room for such an intricate manœuvre," and his arm swept the passage, where at least five men could have walked abreast. "Therefore," he concluded, "our momentum was such that we were unable to avoid collision." As he said these last words the Colonel, to my intense relief, looking somewhat surprised and annoyed, came out and joined us.

The Major knew the Colonel, as did several of the others, and after preliminary bows and heel-clicking of a rather unsteady kind, he was hailed cheerily and two full glasses were passed over the heads in the doorway although not without spilling a good deal upon the said heads, and eventually reached the Colonel and myself. Then everybody was talking, laughing and shouting, and the Colonel, because several of the officers there were senior to himself, had to remain a few minutes out of politeness. When nobody seemed to be looking in my direction I seized the momentary opportunity to slip back to my bedroom.

Here I double-locked the door and rushed to the bed. As I hoped, the Lieutenant had made his escape. One terrible crisis of that night had been got over, anyway. I was not sure what to do next, but I had not long to wait.

The Colonel was knocking on the door and fruitlessly turning the handle.

"Listen, my angel, I am waiting outside. Will you not let me in?" he was urging. "Perhaps it is that you are undressing," he said as an afterthought, "and you would prefer that I wait?"

"Yes, I am undressing," I told him breathlessly.

"Very well, I understand. I will rejoin you later, and go to my friends for one quarter of an hour. *Au revoir*, my dearest dear. We shall meet again very soon," and I heard his footsteps recede up the corridor.

The drink I had gulped down in the other room must have been strong, for my brain was working with a bell-like clearness. All of a sudden, I knew exactly what I was going to do. I would run from the hotel immediately, while the Colonel was in the other room. I had all the information I had wanted. As for my suitcase with the few spare clothes I had brought with me, that could go hang. There was nothing there which could incriminate me.

With the help of my railway pass I should be able to catch a train before dawn for Roulers, and once I was outside the hotel and in public I did not think the Colonel would pursue and cause a scene for reasons I have mentioned.

I scribbled in pencil on a piece of writing-paper:

"HERR COLONEL,

I reserve the right of a woman to change her mind. I was a young and foolish girl; I was carried away by you. Now I am going home, and I hope eventually you will forgive me.

Good-bye,

MARTHA."

Then, seizing my special railway pass and the key of the door, for I had decided to relock it on the outside and keep the key to perplex the Colonel for a few extra minutes while the distance between us widened as much as possible, I tore open the door and dashed straight into the solid grey form which blocked the way. It was the Colonel.

He smiled down at me and explained a little thickly: "My angel, I have just remembered that when I was holding you in my arms in our bedroom, I heard my cigar-case drop to the floor from my breeches pocket. I had come to ask that you would hand it out to me, angel, for I loathe other men's cheap cigars; but, behold, here you come to meet me!" Suddenly the significance of the fact that I was still fully dressed seemed to penetrate his fuddled senses, and he may have noticed the wild look in my face.

"What is the matter, mein Fräulein?" he interrogated, holding me by the shoulders and gently forcing me back through the door. "Where do you go?"

"Please—let me go," I breathed. "I have changed my mind. I am leaving for home.—Please, please—but forgive me. I am frightened, I ought never to have come. I was mad, crazy, but please let me go!"

I tried to slip from his grasp, but he held me firmly, though not unkindly.

"Little one, little one, there is nothing at which to be frightened. Calm yourself. Sit down and I will fetch you a drink." He kissed my forehead tenderly, and I leaned away from him as far as I could as I looked around me wildly, feeling my last chance of escape had gone.

In an alcove of the wall beside the door stood the washhand stand with a basin and ewer of gleaming blue china. I looked up at the Colonel. He was neither intoxicated nor sober. He was not very steady, and I did not think his brain would work quickly. I let my body lie limp against his, with my head resting near his shoulder, then in a flash, I braced my limbs and leaped back with all my strength. I reached the washhand stand, and seizing the blue ewer, launched the whole contents full into the Colonel's eyes before he understood what was happening. He staggered back gasping, and just behind him, as I had calculated, were the two suitcases by the bed-foot. I rushed at him and threw all the weight of my body into a sudden shove. He toppled headlong backwards over the cases and I think his head struck the copper nob of the bed-post.

I turned and catching up my train pass and the door-key which had fallen to the floor, fled from my peacock bedroom, locking the door behind me.

A moment later I was hastening through the darkened and deserted lounge. The night door-keeper wished me a polite good night. It was no business of his, but for all that he must have wondered where a lady guest in the hotel was going at that hour.

One hour and a half later I was lying back in the train, still breathless and incredulous, gliding swiftly through the night towards Roulers.

It was growing late when the train drew into Roulers. A woman passenger on the trains at that time was unusual, but my pass carried me safely through the military police at the barrier. Everybody was still in bed when I reached the café, but presently my mother was embracing me in the doorway. She did not question me as to where I had been. It was enough for her that I had returned safely.

"Canteen Ma' called here yesterday and left this," she told me, slipping a cheap pin-cushion into my hands. The message read:

"No. 63 is absent on a special mission until Thursday. If before that day you have urgent news to transmit you must yourself carry the information to the Van Roots' farm-house along the Thourout-Roulers Road. You will knock at the door with two short and three long raps and hand your message to a fat woman (with a florid complexion) within. You will not allude to the message in any way, but will greet all as acquaintances."

I knew of the Van Roots, trustworthy folk who lived at a lonely farmstead among pine-trees lying nearby the highway. But the distance from Roulers was about fifteen miles by road, and as I could not risk using such a conspicuous route, it meant a journey of almost twenty miles by night over rough countryside. I should have to leave Roulers as soon as darkness fell and make all haste for my destination. The Oberartz must not know of my return to Roulers until after I had come back from delivering my message. I should have overstayed my leave, but I could excuse myself on the grounds of my imaginary grandmother's extreme illness and the fact that I had heard in Brussels that the All Highest would not visit us until Saturday.

I left Roulers at ten o'clock that Wednesday night in a shower of rain and inky blackness. I had only a small torch to guide me and could wear neither coat nor hat, as anyone who had the appearance of having travelled any distance in those days was immediately under suspicion. One always had to look as though one were just running in to see a neighbour, whatever was the real nature of the mission. Food, shelter and if necessary a hiding-place could always be found with Belgians whose homesteads were *en route*, and no questions were ever asked or information ever given to prying German gendarmes, who both in uniform and plain clothes were sometimes to be met with in unexpected places. All along the route to the frontier was a string of farms, private houses, empty ruins and factories which formed a veritable network of relays for the runners with secret and vital information. Here, also, fugitives bound for Holland might lie safely hidden for months. It is when I remember these things, and the unselfish, fearless spirit that was manifested in those War days, that I feel proud of my countrymen.

The old town was only a mile behind me when the moon suddenly glided from behind a cloud, plunging the deserted landscape into a sea of light and shadow. The drizzle ceased and I felt the warmness of the night, but the rain had made the ground slippery and sodden, and the way was wild and strewn with small undulations. I had to break my way through hedges and sometimes had to crawl through ditches, keeping a watchful eye for prowling figures. It was a terribly tiring business, but I cannot honestly say that I disliked it. Once only I saw human beings, and that was when I was crossing a road. It was at a bend where the hedges were high and the road was dark with trees. As I was in the middle of the road an approaching light appeared round the bend. I hurled myself into the waterlogged ditch as a gendarme bicycle patrol swept round the corner.

It was 6 a.m. by my watch when I came on an old house standing by itself, where a light was flickering in the lower windows. I was not certain of the way, so I called at the door to inquire. The aged woman who answered my knock showed no surprise at my muddy, bedraggled condition. She said not a word, but took my hand and led me in, patting my wrist softly. She gave me steaming hot coffee and bread and butter by the fire and then directed me onwards.

When I had walked three-quarter way up the stone-flagged garden path of the Van Roots' homestead, I suddenly noticed beside the wooden porch two muddy bicycles. They were German military bicycles. My heart stood still, and I thought of retracing my steps. Then it occurred to me that to do so would be indiscreet as I might already have been observed from the windows. I advanced boldly to the door as though it was quite a natural thing to be smothered in mud from head to foot, but I thought it prudent to knock on the door like a chance caller and not to use the preconcerted signal. The red-faced fat woman herself opened the door and I greeted her loudly like an old friend. The passage behind her was empty so I quietly rapped out the signal on the door-panel. She nodded, and I passed the note into her hand.

"It shall go immediately," she said, when she saw the "Urgent" with which I had marked it. She glanced over her shoulder. "Two gendarmes on night patrol called here for food," she told me. "They are washing in the scullery. You must come upstairs before they see you, and hide among the rafters."

I stretched myself in the straw of the loft and fell fast asleep. An hour later she told me I might safely come down. After a square meal, which I took basking at a table in the sun-bathed garden, she helped me indoors, washed me in a hip-bath like a small child; during which process I several times fell asleep; and having taken my garments to be brushed and dried, she led me to a feather-bed, into which I slipped blissfully, and closed my eyes.

At ten o'clock that night I started for home. I had determined to spend the next day with friends who lived half-way to Roulers, and to complete the journey the following night. Thus I calculated I could be home at 4.30 a.m. on the Saturday morning, and would have ample time to present myself at the hospital at my usual hour of seven o'clock.

As I set out to the hospital that Saturday morning the air was fresh and enlivening, the birds sang merrily and the sun shone in a blue sky. I tnought of the All Highest sitting silently in his opera box, and wondered if to-day was to be his last. The streets were festooned with gay flags in honour of his coming.

Alphonse was tinkering with the wheel of an ambulance before the steps in the courtyard as I approached. He looked at me searchingly, for although he could not have known where I had been, he may have had a pretty shrewd idea.

"Good morning, sister," he began. "Have you heard the news; it has just been received. The Kaiser is not coming to visit us after all. For the last few days the 'Seven Sisters' have flown over and bombed us regularly, so they have decided that it will be too dangerous for him."

I said nothing, for there was really nothing to be said.

CHAPTER VII

In the autumn "Canteen Ma" brought a warning from over the frontier—"Take care—counter-espionage being tightened up throughout area. Trust no one."

A new battalion had recently arrived and had taken up their quarters in the buildings and outhouses of a disused brewery on the outskirts of the town. They were to stay at Roulers for several days before going up to the line, as many of them were new men fresh from home. The battalion was about one thousand strong, including officers. As a rule, the German troops in Roulers were billeted throughout the whole place in twos and threes, and it seemed to me that one thousand men collected in a small space would afford a target for the "Seven Sisters" that was not to be missed.

The warning about counter-espionage was all very well, but what could one do?—Nothing except hope for the best, for Heaven knows one was careful enough already. Two civilians had been arrested as spies in the town only a fortnight before. They were clients of our café—a well-to-do middle-aged man and his sister—but I had had no idea that they were spies and the secret friends of escaping prisoners until the story of their arrest spread round Roulers. As for the deceitful Otto,

I had become so used to his friendly and confidential ways throughout the summer that I had lost much of my fear for him, for I had determined that he should not learn anything about my activities unless he employed more subtle means than he was using at present; if, indeed, he was employing means to trap me at all.

We were busy at the hospital that night till nearly nine o'clock; but, in case I might be watched, I decided to go straight home and not to deliver my message about the troops in the brewery to No. 63 until later. Actually it was nearly midnight when I slipped past the police patrols and came to the silent alleyway. I was just about to give my usual curious sequence of taps when I heard footfalls in the street; steps which came nearer and then stopped.

Like a flash I was at the far end of the paved court, crouching in the shadow. My heart thudded in my throat. Had I been followed—discovered? I felt my message about the brewery burning against my breast. Had I time to destroy it before they arrested me? Then soft footsteps came down the alleyway towards me and halted just outside the fifth window. It occurred to me as I pressed myself into the shadows that here was another secret agent who used the same "mail bag." A dark form outlined itself against the night, then quite distinctly I heard the same sequence of taps on the glass that I myself gave. Almost I came out of my hiding-place to see who it could be. It was well that I did not. The window slid softly upwards, without noise, as so often it had slid upwards for me. A hand came out from the darkness within, white, outstretched. Then the most amazing thing happened. The shadowy figure pulled something from its belt, there was an infinitesimal pause then a red glare slashed the night, followed by a crash that echoed and re-echoed from the enclosing walls. There came a strangled sob, a horrible scream and then a thud. The figure pushed the window up further and climbed in. For long minutes I crouched with cold fear at my heart. No. 63 had been discovered. No. 63 was now dead. Maybe to-morrow, I, too, should be facing the black muzzles of rifles. That was the penalty of espionage. By a superhuman effort and bending low, I slid past that window of death and crept into the street, shaking in every limb. Ten minutes later I was secure in my own bedroom, wiping the sweat of terror from my face. It had been the worst moment in my whole career. And how was I to get the news through that for three or four days that brewery on the outskirts of Roulers would be crowded with German infantrymen?

In the morning my mother remarked that I had not slept well. It was true. I had not closed my eyes. Then I told her everything.

"Courage," she whispered. "Maybe 'Canteen Ma' will be in the Place to-day. Give me the message, and if I see her I will contrive to slip it into her hand. There will have to be a new line of communication for you." She had more courage than I, that mother of mine. I went to the hospital expecting each moment a hand to fall on my shoulder. But there was no sign. Apparently I was unsuspected still. Yet in that lower room in the silent alley at this moment, No. 63 was lying cold and stiff with a ragged wound in the head. It seemed to me that morning that in some ways No. 63 was the luckier. Only when I returned at night after a seemingly endless day in which everything went wrong, did I obtain news. "Canteen Ma" had been seen by mother in the Place soon after I had left for the hospital, and my mother had followed her to a quiet side-street and slipped the message into her hand while she was gazing into a shop window. My message would be over the Dutch frontier this very night. How I blessed "Canteen Ma"! If ever a woman deserved recognition and honour, that white-haired old pedlar woman did! A load was lifted from my shoulders, for there had grown in me a burning enthusiasm in my calling of spy, just as a soldier feels enthusiasm to fight for what he upholds. Yet that night I could not sleep either.

One thousand men in a dark building waiting unknowingly for death! Over to the east, mothers, wives, pretty girls were even now writing to those men, sending them little presents of home-made jam and sweets—perhaps many of these would arrive too late and would be returned to the broken-hearted senders unopened. And the curtain of smoke and searing steel which was to fall on those light-hearted soldiers was to be lowered by my hands. But this was War.

That evening Otto came up to me in the café. I thought I detected a shifty look about him, for at first his eyes ran round the room rather than meet my own.

"Fräulein, step aside a minute, will you please," he said to me in a low voice, grasping my arm. In fear and trembling I went, for I had no choice but to obey. I forced a smile of inquiry. As we stood at the foot of the stairs, he said:

"Fräulein, I want to speak to you on a very serious matter."—The last vestige of colour left my cheeks. "Will you come to my room, we can be sure of being alone there, at any rate.—Come, you can trust me, we have always been friends."

I nodded, trying not to look amazed, and followed him up the stairs. What in the world did Otto intend to say to me? He did not intend to make improper advances; he was not that type. I had thought at first he was going to arrest me. Did he intend to interrogate and trap me in some cunning way? When he threw the door of his room open and ushered me in I was frightened, but nevertheless throbbing with curiosity and steeled for whatever might happen.

"Be seated, mein Fräulein—a cigarette?" he invited as he pulled a chair forward for me beneath the light. So he intended that I should sit with my face full in the light, while he no doubt would seat himself in a gloomy corner where he could watch the expression on my face at leisure. I took the cigarette, thanked him for the lighted match he proffered, and then flopped down carelessly on the bed, pretending not to have noticed his chair.

Otto drew up a chair by the bedside, and leant his face on his hands.

"Everywhere I hear good reports of you. You can be trusted and have sense, Fräulein," he started. This was surprising. On his face was the ghost of a smile, that old disarming smile; yet I thought of a ferret showing its teeth. "Perhaps you may be surprised to learn that I am a member of the German Secret Service. The question I have to ask you, Martha, is this. Already you have gained the Iron Cross—are you willing to work for the Fatherland—to gain even greater distinction?"

He had spoken coolly, steadily, and his eyes seemed to pierce me. Was this man speaking in all earnestness, or was this some clever trap? I must go warily.

"If you will explain more fully," I rejoined, "perhaps I can help you. What is it you wish me to do?"

He was still watching me closely.

"Yes," he ruminated half to himself, "I will trust you. Fräulein, have you ever had cause to suspect any one of your acquaintance as a spy against Germany?"

I stared at him, hardly believing my ears.

"You may well look surprised, Fräulein," he continued, standing up and beginning to pace to and fro, "but I have certain knowledge that there are at least three dangerous spies in Roulers at this moment. One, a woman, was shot last night, I understand." He was looking at me intensely again. He meant poor No. 63 evidently—so she was a woman like myself. I met his gaze calmly. What was Otto thinking behind those eyes? If only I knew. Could his have been the dark silhouette which had invaded the silent alley last night? Could he have followed me home? Was I on trial without realizing it, and was he waiting for me to betray myself unawares?—What did he know—what did he know? Yet did he know anything? Did he suspect anything?

"Who are these people you suspect?" I asked.

He smiled, and there came into his eyes that look of boyish pride at being in possession of a secret.

"That, Martha, I shall reserve to myself."

"Well, I am waiting for my orders," I reminded him.

Otto then proceeded to give me detailed notes of the men and women I was to watch in Roulers. I did not know whether they were spies or not, although in one or two cases I strongly suspected such to be the case. However, they had nothing to fear from me whatever befell. Apparently neither Alphonse nor Stephan were under suspicion; but then perhaps every word Otto was saying to me in his now seemingly eager boyish way was merely a "blind." Otto wished me to gain the confidence of those Belgians whom he had named to me as being under suspicion. He said that the high authorities looked on Roulers as a regular hotbed of treachery—what insolence these Germans had to use such a word against the enforced slaves of their *Kultur*—he believed that I might be able to tell him something of the organized system of espionage which he knew existed, and which his superiors repeatedly ordered must be checked.

Otto also suspected certain Alsatian conscripts in German uniform, again perhaps rightly, but he could prove nothing against them. It seemed that legal proof that the person was a spy mattered little, so long as the fact that he was acting as a spy could be established. I gathered that one morning such a person might be posted as "missing." That was simple.

"Understand, Martha," he finished, "I want results, and we are prepared to reward handsomely those who produce them. What is happening here is serious. The Higher Command are not pleased with us."

He smiled a little ruefully and gave me another cigarette.

"Martha," he stopped and looked down at me in his frank, almost affectionate way, "you are a very intelligent girl, far more intelligent than most girls—and you are pretty too. I believe you could help us a great deal."

He was caressing my hair with his well-shaped fingers, thoughtfully.

I stood up.

"Herr Otto," I said, "I am going to bed now, and I shall think about what you have said, and the ways in which I can help you."

"Good night, and pleasant dreams, meine liebe Fräulein," he said softly as he opened the door for me. But what was Otto thinking?—What was Otto thinking?

As the door closed behind me I felt like screaming, like beating myself against the wall with agonized suspense. I was in a terrible quandary; against my will I had become a spy for friend *and* foe. But I must bring forward some information for the Germans which would not hurt my friends or the Allies, but which nevertheless would seem of value to Otto. The best way to allay any suspicion which lay on me was to prove my willingness to help the German cause. And I was frightened of a German firing-party in the cold dawn. I must do something. I lay on my bed, turning restlessly, almost weeping with despair, and my brain refused to come to my aid.

Soon after midnight three nights later, I was wakened by the angry droning of the "Seven Sisters" overhead. I wondered what those soldiers in the brewery were thinking about. For all they knew it was just an ordinary raid. A few shattered houses, a few stray casualties, nothing for soldiers to worry themselves about. How they would have scattered like wasps from a disturbed nest had they known that they were the magnet drawing the "Seven Sisters." The anti-aircraft barrage had roared into full blast when I heard the screaming whistle which heralded the descent of the first bomb. Time and again the "Seven Sisters" were caught in the sweep of the searchlights, but the efforts of the German gunners were unavailing. The thud of explosion after explosion followed in rapid succession, and above the din I heard human screams. Then the "Seven Sisters" passed, roaring above in the direction of home.

Half an hour later I was summoned to the hospital. Blood oozed through the mattress to the floor from many a hospital bed that night. Men were crowded moaning in the corridors. I shall never forget the cries of those men. I worked doggedly, dazedly, trying not to remember that I was responsible for the bloody human wreckage around me.

Otto drew me aside next day.

"Fräulein," he said, and his mouth had a tight, unpleasant look. "That bombing of the battalion in the brewery last night was the result of a warning from some spy in this town. I am going to get that spy, Martha. Such vermin must be ground underfoot like beetles, eh? You are going to help me, Martha. I shall hope to hear that you have learned something within a week." And so he left me.

Otto's eyes had told me nothing. Was he waiting to pounce? He wanted results, and if I did not come through his test as an acknowledged helper of Germany—I dreaded to think further. But I could not give what he demanded. I went about hag-ridden with the gnawing fear of that thought. In despair I even thought of bringing forward false evidence against one of their own secret detectives who made the lives of civilians in Roulers such a curse, with their continual insolence and house-to-house searches from which they gained nothing.

"Have you any news for me, Martha?" inquired Otto at the end of the week as he passed me on the stairs one evening. "I think you must have got some inkling of the activities carrying on here by now?" He peered into my face with a cunning, eager expression.

I shook my head.

"I see," he muttered, and then: "Now, Martha, do not be afraid. You understand that in this work not a soul in Roulers will know anything of your part. You may trust me absolutely." There was a pause while he pressed my hand reassuringly. Then he dropped it rather suddenly. "You realize, Martha," he pronounced in a low tone, "that I am perfectly certain that with your knowledge of the civilians of this place you will be able to give me the information I want. If I find that your mind is a blank and you know nothing about these matters, I shall naturally begin to look for a reason.—I have always liked you, Martha. I do not wish to make myself unnecessarily unpleasant." He turned and hurried on down the stairs.

I was staring out of my bedroom window early one morning, watching a fat little robin dancing among the green foliage of the tree without, and thinking how much happier was his lot than mine, when some shots gave me an idea. At the opposite side of the Place, a German soldier in shirt-sleeves was shooting at a pigeon. There was no doubt that in the first days of the War, at any rate, these birds were much used for carrying secret messages, and there was a general order among the military in Roulers that every pigeon was to be shot on sight. There and then I sat down and wrote on a tiny scroll of paper a series of six four-letter numbers, interspersed with letters. This I crumpled and rubbed against a piece of raw meat until it was well blood-smeared. Then I went to the hospital as usual. When the Oberartz made his rounds, I asked him to telephone Otto, and within half an hour an orderly informed me that he was waiting in the office. He was alone.

"You have discovered something?" he exclaimed, regarding me earnestly. "Well Martha, what is it?" Had he asked that question with a slightly ironic note in his voice? I was not sure.

I produced the cryptic message from my pocket.

"I obtained this from a certain Belgian who wishes to remain anonymous," I explained. "He found the bird with this note clipped to its leg lying dead just outside the town, on the road to Ypres. I cannot decode it, but you will note that below the code writing there is a Y3. This represents a signature. I have discovered that all those employed in anti-German espionage in the Roulers area are referred to as the Y group, and each individual of these, of course, has a number. No doubt with your training as a secret service officer you will be able to make more of this than I."

He snatched the paper, pored over it, then straightened up.

"Without, a doubt!" he muttered half to himself. "You have begun well, Martha.—Better than I had expected!—This shall go at once to the cipher department—they can decode any message ever written within forty-eight hours," he finished brightly, and hastened from the room.

So for a moment I had created a respite for myself. It was a blessed relief. I felt like the individual who had just come out from a gruelling afternoon in the dentist's chair with the knowledge that a week was to elapse before he must sit in it again. I might succeed in beguiling Otto for some considerable time if I used all my ingenuity, but I could not carry on upon these lines for ever. This was but a respite. I must rack my brains for some more effective way of combating Otto. For the moment, however, I could feel the joy of peace and security.

A week later I passed Otto talking to a man whom I knew to be a plain-clothes detective in the Place. He saw me and came towards me, touching his cap as if his mind was otherwise occupied.

He was looking at me hard. "I cannot understand it, Martha" he began. "The cipher department cannot make head or tail of that note you handed me. Do you understand the significance of that? It is very strange, for a man well trained in cipher work should in time be able to decipher anything which another man can put into cipher." While he had been speaking, he had been looking upward following the flight of a bird. Swiftly he looked me straight in the eyes. "Martha, do you think that message can have been a 'blind'?" he suggested in a quiet tone.

"I can't tell, Herr Otto," I replied, trying to hide the catch in my breath. "But perhaps we shall learn later."

"H'm—well, we shall see," he grunted. "In the meanwhile, Martha, you will carry on with your investigations, eh?—and I shall hope to have a talk with you before long." He saluted and his smile held no warmth in it, then he turned back to the man he had left.

All that night I was terribly frightened, and once more in the morning at the hospital, I seized a favourable opportunity to tell my fears and troubles to Alphonse. He listened with a grave, worried face until I had finished, then he pushed his hands deep into his pockets and examined the cobblestones in the yard.

"This is a very bad situation, sister," he said. "I am terribly sorry for you, as I can realize what you must have been through. I do not see at this moment what can be done, but I am going to think extremely hard."

"If something does not happen to help me out of this ghastly dilemma soon, I shall go mad or break down and confess everything."

"You will do no good by worrying, little sister," he said kindly.

~

Two days later the dead body of Otto was round lying beside the Menin Road by a transport driver at seven o'clock in the morning. Two bullets had passed through his brain. At first I thought the murder had been done by Alphonse, and for all my relief I was shocked and somehow a little sorry, but later I discovered that on that night Alphonse had been up at the line with his ambulance. Then I asked him about it.

"I think it must have been a 'safety-pin man,' sister," was his answer. "The day after you told me of your trouble I saw the old woman, 'Canteen Ma,' in the town and followed her out of Roulers to a quiet part of the countryside. Then I went up and showed her my safety-pins. I told her of the position you were in. All she said was: 'Well, there are several safety-pin men, good friends of mine, who will be interested to hear this!' And with that she tapped the nag with her stick and on she went."

A tall, moustached stranger approached me one evening not long afterwards as I was walking along a quiet side-street towards home.

"Mademoiselle, would you kindly direct me to the Grand Place" he requested in Flemish.

With a quick glance I saw he was dressed in shabby, work-soiled clothes with muddy boots, as if he had come from a long distance. He wore an old cap at a jaunty angle. His right arm hung stiffly like that of a man who has suffered from a wounded shoulder—and in his left hand was a rank-smelling cigarette.

He smiled, and white even teeth flashed from his good-looking face. "I am looking for the Café Carillon, Mademoiselle," he explained, 'and if you can tell me the way to get there I'll be obliged." He looked an unusual kind of working man, I thought to myself, and what was more, he was looking for my home. I restrained my curiosity.

"If you will walk a little way with me, I'll point the Place out to you, Monsieur," I offered, and we set out together.

I contrived to pilot him well into the centre of the road as we neared the Place, for in those days in Roulers even the walls were likely to have ears.

"The address you ask for, Monsieur, is my home," I informed him.

"Then you are 'Laura'?" he murmured in an undertone.

"You have guessed right."

Making a gesture with his left hand to the lapel of his coat he whispered: "A packet of safety-pins is more expensive to buy now than it was a month ago.—Would you be able to come to the Sturms' farmhouse to-night. I have important news." My late pass would enable me to do the hour's journey to the farm with safety, and I nodded assent. Instinctively I felt that something out of the common was about to happen in connection with this safety-pin man. What impressed me most about him was the deathly pallor of his face and his marked military bearing. He had taken a considerable risk in venturing into the town at all, and I was determined to give him what help I could.

"When we reach the corner leading into the Place, leave me and return to the Sturms," I advised. "I will join you at the farm at eight thirty to-night." At the corner some "knubs" were leaning against the wall outside their billets and the stranger stopped.

"Thank you, nurse," he exclaimed, shaking my hand. "I will tell my mother what you have advised," and, touching his cap, strolled off the way he had come with shoulders hunched and hands in pockets.

I arrived at the farm at 8.30. Madame Sturm I knew; she was the typical Flemish "boeren"—large, hard-working, thrifty, the mother of twelve children, and proud of two sons fighting "on the other side." I had sometimes been of service to her by getting letters through to her sons by "Canteen Ma," and receiving letters from them. She appeared to be expecting me. She did not make any mention, however, of my mission, but showed me into a small sparsely furnished room, where the windows looked out on an enclosed yard. In the half-gloom the stranger was lying on a bed. He stretched out his hand to mine, but did not rise.

"Please sit down, Mademoiselle," he invited, and glancing at him as I obeyed I saw that he looked very ill. He lit one of his rank cigarettes and began to smoke feverishly, and as he smoked, he talked.

"I am a Belgian Officer of the Line," he began, and then in short staccato sentences he told his story. Hearing that a volunteer was needed to obtain first-hand information of the huge "Lengenboom" gun posted outside Moere—the cannon that had shelled Dunkirk and the back areas thirty and forty miles behind the line—he had asked to be given the desperate mission. The district he knew very well and could speak the local dialect fluently.

Dropped by an aeroplane six weeks before outside Pitthem, he at first tried to get work at a farm situated about a quarter of a mile from the gun emplacement. Unfortunately, however, although all his papers were in perfect order, the military would not allow new labourers to commence work in localities so near to the gun. It was then he noticed that gangs of civilian prisoners, most of them under short sentence for petty breaches of the German civil regulations, were daily employed on road-mending in the vicinity of the emplacement. He decided to be arrested. Accordingly that same evening, pretending to be intoxicated, he staggered from a café and upset a very dandified Prussian lieutenant into the gutter. When his infuriated victim rose to curse him for a drunken boor, the Belgian roared that it was entirely his fault, and hurled such a blasting flow of epithets at the scandalized Prussian that the next morning found him cheerfully mending roads on a three weeks' term almost within the very shadow of the great gun.

"It is a tremendous affair, Mademoiselle," he muttered enthusiastically. "There are underground galleries and com-partments for ammunition as big as a church, all buried in cement walls three metres thick, and guarded and patrolled night and day. There are also electrically charged wires all round the position which one has to be careful to avoid."— Then he added quietly, "I have orders to destroy it." I caught my breath. What a mad undertaking!

"My official number is '8,'" the man on the bed went on, "and my name is Edmund, so should I get 'pipped,' as is more than possible, please let the proper quarter know, as there are several friends of mine who would like to have a try at this job." His voice had fallen away to a whisper, a jaunty whisper albeit, and I saw pain twisting his face.

"What is the matter with you?" I questioned anxiously. "Have they 'pipped' you as it is?"

"We used to sleep in a hut not far from the emplacement. Our guards were old soldiers and not over strict. Three nights ago I managed to climb through a window of the hut and explore. They are lazy devils, those gunners, at night-time. I had just started mapping out the position for the information of the airmen in case I was not able to blow the thing up when an infantry patrol challenged me. I ran for it—in the wrong direction, too, so as to put them off the scent, and in the darkness I got clean away, doubled back and climbed through my window, but a bullet got me through the shoulder. I hid the wound from the sentries, and later that day, as my term was up, they let me go"—while he talked, I had hastily torn off the rough bandages made of old shirt twisted round his shoulder, and found it to be a deep flesh wound, much inflamed.

"It's lucky the bullet passed right through my shoulder or else I should have been forced to chance a visit to a doctor. I missed a few awkward questions there, nurse, eh?" he exclaimed lightly, although his mouth twitched.

"Now, Edmund No. 8," I admonished severely, "you will rest here for another five days, at least, and give yourself a chance to get back your strength. Meanwhile I will think what can be done to give the 'Lengenboom' its marching orders."

"Remember, 'Laura,' this 'Lengenboom' business is my pigeon, not yours.—I have come a long way to pay a visit to that old gun, you know!—For all that, when I'm well again I'll hope for your assistance in doing the trick."

"I shall wait to hear from you," I assured him. "Good night, Edmund No. 8, and may our next meeting be a luckier and more exciting one."

So I left the farmhouse, giving Madame Sturm instructions as to the dressing of Edmund's shoulder. Ypres was a red glow in the western sky, and the distant roar of the guns seemed almost a part of nature.

Four evenings later a small boy ran past me and slipped a note into my hand as I was returning home. He was one of the children of Madame Sturm. Burning with curiosity I hastened to my bedroom.

"Meet me at 'Den Paard' Café, Wynendale, at 6 p.m. to-morrow—given a little help from you, the 'pin' may fit— No. 8," I read, and that night and during my work the next morning I was full of excitement. No one could desire a more staunch and gallant companion for any desperate enterprise, I thought to myself.

"Den Paard" Café was one of those large café-farms common in Flanders, lying between Thourout and Wynendale, the latter a village close to Moere. I had about twelve kilometres to go, and was fortunate in a double sense to obtain a lift in a passing farmer's trap which was going in the direction of Moere. It was a wet afternoon, but for that I was thankful because the hood of the trap hid me from the watchful eyes of the inquisitive military patrols.

My companion was a fat, dreary-looking individual, with drooping grey moustaches, who only interrupted his continual grumblings against the "bloody Boches" to give an occasional irritable flick with his whip to the glistening back of his sleepy pony, who seemed quite at ease in the downpour. Apparently the farmer had just had his finest mare confiscated by "knubs" to drag their wretched transport. It was evident that this was a very sore point;— ransack his farm for "hoardings," imprison his labourers for ridiculous offences, to be the victim of light-fingered soldiery; all this was in the day's work, but the so beautiful mare was another matter. And so the dreary tirade went on.

I found myself growing distinctly nervous as we neared the scene of the rendezvous, as if something unexpected was about to happen. The trap had reached to within two hundred and fifty yards of the farm buildings when I saw the tall figure of Edmund leap through the door of the café into the roadway. Another figure in civilian clothes dashed after him. Edmund made across the road, vaulted the fence into the low fields, and then quick as thought he whipped round, and two reports crashed out. A figure was sprawling grotesquely by the steps, and Edmund No. 8 was springing over the fields to a thick clump of trees, leaving a blue wisp of smoke from his revolver hanging on the air.

Then suddenly from the further end of the farm a second figure, revolver in hand, and bending double for cover as he darted along the hedges, started in hot pursuit of Edmund. I had instinctively laid my hand on the driver's arm, stopping his horse. We waited in the deepening shadows of the trees, the horse nervously pawing the ground.

The pursuer had vanished among the trees. Shots echoed from the wood, then silence, then shots more distant, and once again the evening silence. We waited for a time that seemed an eternity to me, my companion saying not a word, but seeming to accept it all as a matter of course, when to my unutterable relief I saw the second man break through the bushes on the outskirts of the wood and walk painfully towards the café with his left hand supporting his right arm. He passed slowly within less than a hundred yards of the trap, but was too occupied with the blood running over his forearm to notice us in the falling gloom. So Edmund escaped again.

When the wounded agent had reached the café the farmer looked at me hard, but I do not think my face reflected much my agitation.—"Well," he shrugged, "such is life in occupied territories, and now do you wish to come farther with me, mademoiselle?"—I told him that I had friends whom I had set out to visit living in one of the big houses which dotted the countryside some distance from the main road, left his trap with thanks, and started over the fields to a big house some distance away. Even if he did not believe me, this was safer, especially as I might be watched from the café windows.

As soon as I saw I was alone on the landscape, I turned towards Roulers and began the rough and tiring tramp across country in the now fast-gathering darkness. I had deemed it wisest to return to Roulers, for Edmund was almost certain to make for the Sturms' farm. I might perhaps meet him on the way back. So with my heart thumping at every unusual sound, I made my way home, but neither Edmund nor anyone else came near me in the darkness.

Walking to the hospital the next morning the same small boy ran past me and slipped a note in my hand. I read it when I was inside the shelter of the hospital gates.

"No. 8 is desperately hurt. He is concealed at the Sturms' farmhouse and wishes to speak with you."

I went through my work with a heavy heart that day and as soon as it was finished I seized my cape, and regardless of risk, made my way to the Sturms with all speed.

Madame Sturm met me and, taking a lantern, led me across the farmyard to one of the outhouses. Up the wooden ladder inside we went, and there in the loft, made as comfortable as possible on a bed of hay, was poor Edmund No. 8.

I saw at a glance that he was past all hope. His wound was a great jagged rent across the breast, caused by a ricochet bullet from a revolver. It had been the chance and parting shot of the German agent.

In gasping whispers he blurted: "Well, sister, they didn't get you the other evening—that's good—seems that luck is not on my side—still, I'll polish off the 'Legenboom' yet—just wait till I'm well again—you'll find a packet of cigarettes under the pillow; light one for me, please, and take one yourself." He paused half-smiling, but I knew he was suffering severely.—"It happened this way. The day before last, despite your orders, sister, I'm sorry to say, I went on the prowl, and after dark managed to smuggle myself in among a gang of civil prisoners who were barracked near the 'Legenboom.' I had decided to take a chance and dynamite the H.E. Compartments, hoping that the shells stored there would blow up the whole place, but I wanted to learn a bit more about the insides of the emplacement first, and I also wanted to complete the plan at which they interrupted me the time before—as that would be some help to the others in case I failed.—As I was getting out a sentry challenged and fired—I dashed through a patrol in the darkness, and seemed to have got clean away.—But next day when I went out I found two doubtful-looking civilians were dogging me wherever I went. I thought I had given them the slip and communicated with you."—He paused, begged for water, which he drank greedily, and then continued—"I intended to do the job to-night, and asked you to meet me yesterday in hopes you could arrange an aeroplane diversion, at some time fixed between us, while I got to work below—I was waiting at the café for you—lucky you didn't turn up," and he made a brave attempt to smile. "Then two German secret service men arrived and began to cross-question me. I believed they were the men who had been following me and I expected to be arrested at any moment, for I had on me the complete layout of the position, and also several sticks of dynamite."— Another painful pause.—"I was mortally afraid, too, that you might appear at any moment, so when one of the agents went searching at the back of the café, I tried a bolt for it— then the shooting happened just when I thought I had safely escaped, stopped a stray bullet—a farm labourer hid me and helped me back here during the night." His voice had grown noticeably weaker, but he still wore that half-smile on his face, and had not realized his failing strength himself.

"Now, sister," he added, "mind you don't go blowing up the 'Legenboom' while I'm ill. This is my job—this is my job." Half an hour later Edmund No. 8 was dead—another hero, unhonoured, unsung.

∽

I took the plans of the 'Legenboom' from his shabby old jacket and sent them over the frontier. There were several air attacks on it, but I never heard that much damage had been done, nor did I ever hear of any other adventurers like Edmund No. 8. The two sticks of dynamite I kept, for it seemed to me they were useful articles for a spy to possess, and certainly they were to come in useful enough later on.

CHAPTER VIII

It was on Christmas Eve 1915 that I witnessed one of those tragic sidelights on modern war, a situation old as the hills, yet utterly devastating. A wounded Belgian boy had been brought in a week previously. I think he had been a liaison officer. Always he spoke of his pretty sister in Roulers, whose husband, Jacques, was in the fighting line. It was "Fifine" this, and "Fifine" that, all the blessed day, till I grew tired of her name and the boy's pleading that she should be allowed to come and see him.

"Ask the Oberartz," said the boy. "You are our Little Mother here. He will refuse you nothing."

So at last, as a concession, the favour was granted. Fifine was coming, and the boy would give and hear the latest news of the family. He was in the seventh heaven of delight. So we walked head first into a tragedy which I shall remember to my dying day. Fifine arrived that morning. With her was a German official, uniformed and carrying a revolver at his belt.

"My darling," whispered the girl, rushing to the bedside and covering her brother with kisses. "Say you are not badly hurt. No? An arm only? Thank the good God!"

The boy sat up in bed, frowning.

"Who is that damned fellow?" he muttered quite audibly. "Send him away, Fifine."

The girl grew crimson, while the official stepped forward.

"Permit me to explain," he said, clicking his heels and bowing stiffly from the waist. "Fifine and I are—how do you say—good companions, no? We have arranged these things." He gave an odious smirk. "If you will allow me, I should like to make you a little present."

Then as the Belgian's face grew pinched and grey he laid a hundred mark note on the bedspread! For one interminable moment there was silence. I could hear an orderly in another ward shouting to someone, the tramp of feet on the road outside. I could have shrieked at the agonizing tension. We were all automatons, frozen things playing out our part in a grim tragedy. Then the Belgian broke the spell. The blood rushed to his face. His eyes started from his head.

"You filthy seducer!" he shouted. "You damned swine! Take that—that—!"

In one second he had leaned forward and snatched the revolver from the German's holster. Two shots he pumped into the official's stomach at less than two-foot range. Someone snatched the smoking weapon from the boy's hand, for he was trying to shoot himself as well. The German was screaming on the floor, covered already with blood, while the girl was huddled against a cupboard moaning, her hands over her face. Orderlies ran in, took the official away and placed the boy under arrest. I expected to see him shot on the spot. Fifine I never saw again, and in ten minutes the German was dead. The Belgian was afterwards court-martialled and sent to Germany as a prisoner, a fate for him maybe worse than quick death. I wonder if Jacques ever returned safe and sound from Germany and what Fifine said to him?

I left the hospital dazed, shocked, oblivious of the snowflakes which were beating down fast. The keen air soon revived my spirit, and presently I was re-emerging from the door of our café into the icy blast, with a bundle held under my cloak. I had a job on hand, and that was to smuggle food to hungry civil prisoners in the gaol, for released prisoners had reported that official rations were pitiably meagre.

The prison consisted of a large cellar, the grated windows of which were raised a few inches above the street-level, and in the glass of these were bored holes about two inches in diameter for ventilation. By rolling food into long cylinders, bread and meat could be passed through these holes. Each evening also, hot soup was poured through a tin tube in the same way. Several other girls besides myself had undertaken this task, and we each carried out our supply work one night a week.

In charge of the prison at night were a Feldwebel and one soldier. These took turn in patrolling the building once every two hours. Now the two old Feldwebels who were in charge of the civilian prisoners under the Town-Major were Feldwebels Richter and Jugo, who lived in our house. From the "all-conquering hero" attitude of 1914, with an aloof suspicion and contempt for the subdued inhabitants of Belgium, the tone of the rank and file of the German Army had greatly changed, and most were only too willing to be on friendly and even sympathetic terms with the civilians. The key to this riddle was hunger and want of every description. But officialdom was still harsh and indeed Prussian; remaining so until the end.

Feldwebels Richter and Jugo took turns about by months in carrying out day and night duties superintending the prisoners. Once they had been typical German drill Feldwebels, brutal, officious, and overbearing. A stock joke among the troops in Roulers told how Richter, who was something of a character, had been a great spy catcher at the beginning of the War, and that on one occasion he had raided a nunnery and accused the nuns of being French officers in disguise. Protests were of no avail, and the horrified nuns were ordered to parade before Feldwebel Richter and remove all their garments to prove this was not the case!

But that had been in the days when he had had more food inside him; and, besides, the task of guarding civilians who for the most part had committed no offence at all was not a congenial one. It was no uncommon sight to see Richter—or Jugo—striding home in patched uniforms and down-at-heel "pipes" in rear of their prison squads with a pleased smile of semi-inebriation on his face. Had you gone to their place of work you might not have found a full day's complement done, for the squad spent much of their day sitting round a table in some secluded nearby café, playing cards and treating their keeper to glasses of *Schnapps*, while they took turns to keep watch for inquisitive officers outside. Richter and Jugo had no objection to prisoners being fed and given tobacco at night provided they also got a little, and if they understood that we intended to do no more than feed prisoners they were ready to wink an eye and turn the other way.

It was a standing joke in Roulers that almost every man, woman and child had at one time or another been imprisoned for some petty offence. It had come to be looked upon as quite an honour; in fact, there was almost "something the matter with you" if you did not know the inside of Roulers civil gaol! For instance, there were three small girls, the eldest not more than twelve years old, who were sent to prison for ten weeks for picking up stray pieces of coke lying along the railway, and the Capoardhoeks, a septuagenarian couple who served the same punishment for hiding away a few pounds of potatoes and a little crushed maize.

The commonest and vilest form of crime in German eyes was food smuggling, for the food situation had grown truly serious. House-to-house searches were constant, and people might have to leap out of bed in the middle of the night to let officious gendarmes in to turn everything upside down. Farmers racked their brains for ruses for keeping their crops and livestock. Several served long sentences for rearing of pigs in cellars.

But eighty-year-old Madame Veldhock managed to fool all the gendarmes, and kept the trick going all through the War. She had a beautiful sleek goat called Silina, which she loved passionately, quite apart from Silina's fine milking capacity. The old woman's house was No. 20, and attached was No. 21. Silina lived in the cellar and the old lady had a hole knocked through the wall into the cellar of No. 21. Whenever the searchers banged at the door of No. 20, Silina was bustled through the hole into No. 21, and when they passed on to No. 21 the bewildered goat was hurried bleating back into No. 20. Eventually Silina became so used to this, and her hearing so acute, that every time a visitor called at No. 21 she trotted into No. 20 without waiting for any orders!

There was a "knub" whom I had looked after when he had been lying wounded at the hospital, and every other day he used to push a handcart with medical supplies into Iseghem. Rumour reached me that a man in Iseghem had somehow come by three large sacks of coffee, and that my soldier friend with the handcart knew all about it. He did, and after his next trip brought me two kilos (4½ lbs.), for which he asked £7 10s., and I am confident he was perfectly honest in his demands. He told me that the German military lorry driver who had originally carried the sacks through the patrol to Iseghem had been paid 1000 marks for his trouble by the Belgian tradesman. That delicious coffee we used to drink in a corner of one of the back bedrooms well away from the window, for if the smell of coffee had reached the inquisitive nostrils of some official in the street there would be trouble. This was by no means an isolated instance of German troops conniving to help Belgian civilians in smuggling; provided, of course, they were allowed a share of the proceeds themselves.

Butter, on the rare occasions when I could get it, used to cost about £2 10s. per 2¼ lbs. Food substitutes were in daily use amongst us and a civilian who had thought out a new edible substitute immediately found himself a popular figure. A compound of roasted oat-chaff and roasted pea-shells was commonly nicknamed coffee and sparingly sugared potato pulp answered for jam.

Clothing offered us another problem. Garments and suits were manufactured from bed blankets, canvas blinds and tablecloths and curtains and sheets were made into lingerie. I had made for myself quite dainty ensembles from these uncouth materials. All the drapers' shops had had their stocks commandeered, and it was impossible to get fresh goods, for the Germans seemed determined to use everything of every colour and every material for sandbags.

Roulers was no longer full as it had been when we first arrived little less than a year ago from Westroosebeke, for most of the refugees had moved farther from the lines, and now every day some of the old residents were following them. It was my father and mother's view that the nearer to the fighting lines we were the better, so that when the big push finally came and the Huns were rolled back by the victorious armies of the Allies we should be all the sooner in the arms of our own people and free of the yoke.

It was that snowy Christmas Eve of 1915 that a second incident happened of a surprising character, which I always see enacted over again whenever there is snow on the ground. I had finished giving supplies to the prisoners and as I approached the Place the sound of men's voices cheering lustily rang out. Then followed an intermittent crackle of rifle-fire, straggling away and renewing itself raggedly, accompanied by the gathering roar of voices. Véry lights ripped the night. I was amazed; the only explanation I could think of was a mutiny among the troops. Christmas was a big festival with the Germans, and there had been much unsteady singing and raucous laughter floating from the houses around the Place when I had gone out earlier.

The Place was thronged with yelling "knubs" in every stage of *déshabillé*, despite the falling snow and the crispness of the air, brandishing flaming Christmas trees pilfered from some coppice, linked arm in arm and dancing clumsily in their heavy boots, or shooting wildly into the air. There were officers there, too, and the few bewildered military policemen seemed at a discount. I slipped across to the café without anybody trying to molest me, and just as I was mounting the steps the door suddenly flew open and out dashed Fashugel. A battered spiked helmet balanced drunkenly over one ear, his glove-like tunic was buttoned to its choker collar, but his lower limbs were clad only in his white woollen underpants and socks badly in need of darning. Round his head he brandished a mop. Most of the men billeted nearby belonged to the 52nd M.–G. Coy., and the startling apparition of their gallant Hauptmann was greeted with a roar of delight.

At an adjoining house lived the Brigade Major, and he had apparently been employed on late duty, for his charger, covered with a blanket, was standing outside the house, held by the groom. Suddenly Fashugel gave a whoop and with a wild leap was on the startled horse's back. As soon as he had got his balance, for he nearly fell off the other side, he banged the animal with the mop and shouting at the top of his voice, clattered off into the darkness with the men of the 52nd hurrahing at his heels, firing rifles and revolvers as they ran. It was the news that Serbia had been finally and utterly crushed, added to assurance by the higher authorities that Russia had been rendered ineffective and France was on her last legs, which had prompted this outburst.

I did not see Fashugel again that night, although the revelry in the Place went on for hours. I think perhaps he felt rather ashamed of himself and crept home quietly in the dawn. Certainly the account of his ride round the town was an oft-told tale for many a day.

Two days later the following Garrison Order appeared:

AMMUNITION, WASTE OF:

"It is strictly forbidden to use ammunition to celebrate any National Feasts or Victories of our Glorious Armies in the Field. Commanders will see that this order is strictly adhered to. It is understood that certain officers encouraged the men by a personal example on the demonstration on the night of 24/12/15. In future such conduct will be severely dealt with."

Fashugel never mentioned the episode of Christmas Eve, but I wondered what he thought about it.

It was, of course, only very occasionally that wounded Allied prisoners were brought into the Roulers Hospital and, as a rule, these were evacuated to the rear long before they had reached the convalescent stage. Prisoners who escaped over the Dutch frontier, with the help of the civilians along the line of posts, were men who had succeeded in getting out of the concentration camps elsewhere. The only escape which had been made from the hospital had been that of Jimmy and Arthur which I had effected early in the year. But the opportunity had arisen again. The two prisoners I intended to help were William, a Cockney in a London regiment, and a Corporal Timmins. In neither case had their wounds actually reached the official convalescent stage, but they were both sturdy men who, I believed, would be willing and capable of putting up with a good deal for a chance of liberty.

Christmas, as I have pointed out, was a big festival with the Germans, for although there was not much food about, there was still plenty of liquor, and I thought that in the revelry which was sure to take place during the latter part of Christmas, even so far as was allowed within the hospital, the prisoners would have a better chance of slipping away unobserved than at any other time.

One of my greatest terrors during the time I worked as a spy was that some unforeseen chance might betray me, for you cannot live a double life for months without taking grave risks. In war-time, two and two make a lightning four, and there were a number of civilians who had seen me on mysterious missions. There had been several betrayals in the surrounding districts. I believe unintentional betrayals tricked out of unfortunate captives, but for all that, the less one knew about one's fellow-spies and the less they knew about you, the better. That was why I determined as far as possible to carry through the escape of the prisoners without the help of those outside.

Having warned William and Timmins of my intention, I despatched a note to "Canteen Ma" that I wanted an agent to meet a woman and two men on the outskirts of Lophem by an inn at twelve midnight, on the 25th, and to conduct the two over the frontier. Since the death of No. 63, my new line of communication with those over the frontier consisted in passing my note across the counter of a small chemist's shop situated not far from the Place. Lophem was about fourteen miles distant, and I had an aunt who lived there. As it was imperative that I should show myself at the hospital at the normal hour on the morning after the escape, I asked "Canteen Ma" to call at my aunt's house with her cart at 1 a.m. on the 26th, and as her old horse was a good beast, I expected to reach my home between five and six o'clock.

A few days later I heard from "Canteen Ma" that all would be well, and an agent would be expecting us on the appointed night. She also told me of a certain house with three gables situated in an isolated stretch on the Lophem road, beside a clump of trees, about five hundred yards beyond the tenth kilometre stone from Roulers. This held a secret room by a large fireplace, which was at times used as a resting-place by escaped prisoners on their way to the frontier. She gave instructions as to how to gain the hidden chamber, and warned me that it was unwise to remain in the house without making use of the chamber, as the gendarme patrols sometimes searched disused houses on the road or flashed their torches in through the windows when they knew prisoners were making for the frontier.

Owing to this risk of search by gendarmes, a second exit to the chamber had been constructed. This consisted of a trapdoor in a corner of the floor which led by means of a shaft to the cellars, and from thence a person could reach the open air by a grating. I warned the two soldiers to slip out of the hospital after dusk on the afternoon of the twenty-fifth. In a corner of the civilian staff hut they would find two bundles of civilian clothing and a torch which I had bought, waiting for them. When the civilian employees left at five o'clock they were to walk out of the gates with them, as though nothing were the matter.

Swathed in a rough dark coat, and with my head tied in a handkerchief like a peasant woman, I waited in the shadow at the mouth of a narrow lane till the stream of civilian employees came past from the hospital gate. Then I saw the two Englishmen come out, looking this way and that. They might have been typical Flemish labourers. They had succeeded in putting the hospital gates behind them, at any rate! I turned and hastened for the Thourout Road and the deserted house with the three gables, for I meant to be there first.

As it was not yet the curfew hour a gendarme who passed me on the road did not stop to question me. I hoped the two Englishmen somewhere behind in the darkness would fare as luckily. At 7.20 I stood looking up the dark shadow of the gabled house. It looked eerie through the snowflakes and the silence was absolute.

The little door in the left gable opened easily enough and switching on my torch I found myself in a bare, spacious room where some of the floorboards and much of the wood panelling on the walls were crumbling away with rot. There is an awful sense of loneliness in such a spot at night, and I hoped the Englishmen would arrive quickly. A great open stone fireplace surmounted by a dusty carved overmantel stood opposite me, and at each side of this there showed in panelling the door of a six-foot cupboard which had been let into the wall. Following "Canteen Ma's" instructions, I tried the knob of the right-hand cupboard and it opened with a creak of rusty hinges. Inside I saw the ordinary wooden interior of a big cupboard. Stepping into the cupboard I bent and pushed hard against the back wall of the cupboard near the bottom. I felt the bottom giving inwards, and at the same time the top swung outwards. Throwing the ray of my torch under it, I continued to press the base until the rear wall had swung parallel with the floor, evidently suspended on a pivot passing across its centre at the back. Peering within, I could see the floor of a fair-sized room covered with hay. This false wall was a massive oblong of solid oak. It had worked on its pivot with absolute silence.

I went back into the panelled room and peered through a chink in the boarded windows into the night. It was five minutes after the half-past when two figures flitted by and I heard the creaking of the side-door. Then there were footfalls in the room. For one moment I was frightened to switch my torch on the intruders, for they might have been gendarmes, but a strained voice hissed: "Who's that?"

"All right," I reassured them, "it's I."

"Well, thank Gawd for that, anyway," sighed my interrogator. "Well, what 'appens next, nurse?"

"Follow me," I said, and turning on my torch, entered the cupboard.

"'Ere, how long 'ave we got to stay in this cupboard, nurse?" put the surprised voice of William, when the three of us were safely shut inside. "I'd feel safer if I was away over the frontier instead of playing hide-and-seek with nothing in this ruin."

"It's all right fer you, Will, you didn't take one through the leg like wot I did. I'm ready fer a rest, I am.—Still, I don't see wot cause we got to crush in 'ere when we got the whole 'ouse to lie about in——"

"Well, you will soon," I assured them. "Now get down on your knees, or something is going to hit you hard on the head, and then crawl after me."

They followed me silently under the swinging panel, and a moment later we were sitting on the soft bed of hay on the floor of the secret chamber, the panel stood upright behind us, and I had shot bolts at the top and bottom into sockets in the lintel, so that it could no longer be pushed in from outside.

"Guess wot I put my hand on, nurse," exclaimed the Corporal. "It's an old carriage lamp—and what more it's got the good 'alf of a candle left unused in it," he went on when I flashed my light on his find. "Looks as if someone must 'ave been 'ere not so long ago." He proceeded to light the candle and gaze round our apartment.

"Crikey," muttered William, "a real 'idden chamber with a secret panel, lantern an' all. Feel like a blinkin' Guy Fawkes, I do. Who'd 'ave thought when I was emptyin' dustbins in Poplar, I'd ever be muckin' around in a 'aunted mansion in Flanders?"

"The only sort of ghosts you are likely to find in this vicinity are prowling gendarmes," I told him. "But I think we are pretty safe in here."

I produced from a big pocket which I had had sewn inside my coat three bottles of beer, some bread and goats' milk, cheese, two clay pipes, and some tobacco. William and the Corporal were delighted, and having swallowed the food and drink with cheerful gusto, lay back comfortably in the hay and got their pipes burning.

"Well, I'm for a doze, nurse," said Corporal Timmins, and presently both men appeared to have fallen asleep. It was warm in here in the hay after the piercing cold outside, and I felt rather sleepy myself. I, too, must have fallen into a doze, for suddenly I awakened, hearing voices near at hand, and they were German voices. There was a small grating high up on one of the walls letting air into the chamber from some hidden aperture. The men were outside, and they must be gendarmes. I had seized the two soldiers and shaken them and all three of us were sitting listening anxiously. The voices slowly died away.

"Looks like that wos only a passing patrol, nurse," William broke the silence.

"Ho' much longer we got 'fore we gets moving?" asked the Corporal.

"Five minutes," I told him.

"Better give 'em time to get well clear before we go," he said drily. Quarter of an hour passed, and as there was no further sound, we decided to move. William refilled his pipe and lit it.

"May as well smoke as much of this tobacco as possible before I get caught," he muttered philosophically, and Timmins raised the panel and crept underneath. I heard the creak of hinges as he opened the cupboard door. Then came a startled oath and a guttural voice shouted, "Hey, stop. Who the devil's that?" and with a gasp Timmins scrambled madly back under the panel.

"Gendarmes—two of them—sitting in the room taking shelter—walked right on top of them," he breathed, slamming the panel and reshooting the bolts. Someone was in the cup board, cursing and banging the wall with a hard instrument. Then followed two deafening explosions.

"Gawd, they're shootin'—trapped, my Gawd!—not a hope," muttered William hurling himself on the floor and dragging me with him. Timmins was crouched to one side and they were pumping bullets through the panel now—

"There's another way out," I shouted—"a trap-door somewhere in a corner under the hay——"

"Take care of that tobacco, Will," yelled Timmins frantically, but it was too late. William's pipe had fallen out of his mouth, and the red-hot heart of the tobacco had rolled out into the hay. It began to blaze. I screamed with terror, for I thought that the end had come. Oblivious of bullets William and Timmins rushed at the corners of the room and began tearing up the hay. The centre of the room was a roaring furnace, and the smoke was choking us. The heat was maddening.

"Here's the trap," screamed Timmins in the far corner. "Nurse, pull it up quick and get down—Will, help me to kick all the hay towards the panel."

Gallantly the two men attacked the blazing hay. The trap had a ring in it and when I pulled it rose easily. Below was a black, narrow shaft and a rope suspended from a ring in the side disappeared down it. I threw my legs in, caught the rope and lowered myself into the blackness hand over hand. There was the sound of heavy breathing, and feet kicked my head. The others were following. Then the light from above vanished altogether and I heard the trap close. A few seconds later my feet touched hard ground. The three of us stood in the darkness of the cellar.

"There is a grating we can get out by somewhere and we've got to find it quickly, because before long the flames will attract all the patrols for miles around as well as all the troops in passing vehicles," I said, flashing the ray of my torch round the ceiling. Round and round travelled that ray of light but no signs of a grating appeared, while the minutes sped by.

"Well—if there ain't a grating we'll be roasted alive, even if the ceiling don't drop in on us," murmured William.

I searched the ceiling again, but there was no grating.

"Turn the torch on the walls," ordered Timmins. "I thought so," he said, "the cellar is in two compartments."

My torch had revealed a square aperture in one of the walls. We rushed through, and this time an iron grating showed a ray of light when it reached the far side of the ceiling. Beneath the grating were two wooden boxes, one on top of the other, by which it could be reached.

"I'll go first to see that the coast is clear," murmured Timmins, jumping up on the boxes and pushing his shoulder against the grating. It gave outwards and he threw it aside, thrusting his head cautiously into the opening. There was a pause, for a moment, then he called:

"It's all right, but come quickly, and the moment you're out, run hard to your right—the gendarmes are standing outside at the opposite end of the house, but they are not looking this way—and the flames have got going properly in the lower rooms."

"Don't wait to help me," I urged. "I can manage—one of you may as well escape at any rate, so disappear into the darkness before they turn round."

I helped William up next as the wounded shoulder made climbing difficult, and at one point I heard him groan. He peered anxiously down when he was clear of the hole.

"Are you all right, nurse?" he whispered.

"Yes, run away——"

Then my head and shoulders were through the hole. How blessed the cut of the wind and the touch of the snow felt on my cheeks! I was at the foot of the right-hand gable tower. The whole side of the house and the neglected wilderness of snow-covered garden stood out in flickering light. The woodwork of the lower rooms, especially at the far end of the house near the hidden chamber, was disappearing in a roaring mass of flames. Gazing up at the gable tower stood the two gendarmes, their revolvers still dangling from their hands, and two other soldiers had joined them. Perhaps they thought that whoever had been the mysterious beings in that hidden chamber, they had been burnt alive; perhaps they expected that we had somehow escaped from the flames to the roof and might appear there screaming for aid in the heart of the bonfire, at any minute.

I darted away into the kindly darkness, and presently William and Timmins had joined me, and together we ran, not considering direction, so long as we carried ourselves away from the flaming house. I stopped breathlessly, for I heard the two men, who were keeping up with me gamely, grunt painfully when the uneven ground jolted them.

"What a fool I am," I exclaimed. "I'm sorry, I was frightened, and only wanted to put the house behind me—we have been running away from the frontier."

Turning my torch to my watch, I found that only thirty-eight minutes had elapsed since we had awakened from our doze to hear German voices passing the secret chamber.

"We've got to reach Lophem by midnight, for there I shall give you over to the care of another agent," I explained to them—"we can do it all right but you will have to keep a good pace—are your wounds paining you much?"

"We'll manage it, nurse," said William.

"We must get back to the Thourout Road," I said, "for it is far too dark to risk cutting across country here. We might walk in circles."

The house was a twinkling ball of light which reddened the sky.

"Using that as our guide," I pointed out, "we can make a detour, and strike the road beyond it. There may be gendarmes and passing traffic, and even if the district has not been warned that prisoners are making for the frontier, it is after curfew, and we are bound to be stopped, if seen."

We reached the road about half a mile beyond the house, which was now furiously burning everywhere.

"What time is it, nurse?" asked Timmins.

"We have three hours in which to make Lophem," I told him.

The two men were now limping badly, although considering they had just come from a month at hospital on poor rations, it was amazing how they were standing the wear and tear. They received what I had said in silence and followed me steadily. We had about six and a half miles to cover with our faces to the storm.

A swiftly approaching light showed through the curtain of snow ahead, and we leaped into the mouth of a side lane, as two gendarmes, muffled to the neck, went by on bicycles. Another light was coming up from behind, and as the two passed, we heard them shout to each other. The oncoming patrol sped past in the direction of Lophem—did they know of our escape, and was the countryside being combed for us? Directly they were out of sight, we went on.

On our right two lights showed—I could make out trees beside the way, and I knew that we must presently turn off from the main road to reach Lophem. At that very moment there came a grinding of gears, and a staff car rushed up from behind, seemingly almost on top of us.

"Into the ditch," growled Timmins, seizing me.

Five seconds later we were huddled there with our noses buried in slushy snow, our lower limbs submerged in icy water, for the ice had given way, and our only protection from the subdued glare of the headlights, a low ridge which road-menders had thrown up.

"The dirty devils!" I heard William mutter, "What couldn't I do with a nice little bomb now!"

Long before my heart had ceased thudding in my throat, the Germans were out of sight. We clambered out, feeling utterly miserable, and the wind played through us, and froze our wet garments. William's wound had begun to bleed, but he urged me not to trouble about it, Timmins had gone dead lame now, and had to lean on us both in order to get along. The remainder of that journey was a nightmare, as we crawled along a slushy, pot-holed by-road. I, too, was limping and tired-out, for I had had a heavy day in the wards and was not used to long walking. But they were great boys, those two, and began to hum some English song about a "Long, Long Trail"; in fact, now that they had greatest cause for misery, they were more jesting and cheerful than they had been during the whole tramp.

We were too weary to be cautious now, we just ploughed our way on. There was not a light to be seen, but at last I realized we were nearing Lophem. As a matter of fact, we should have missed the inn altogether had not a man emerged from the darkness and stood staring at us—a German patrol, the thought flashed on me for one ghastly moment. Then he moved forwards.

"Friends for the frontier?" he murmured, pitching his voice low.

I gasped with relief.

"Two friends, yes. Is all well?" He came closer, peering at the Englishmen.

"Good, let us waste no time. They will follow me to the barn, and in the loft can sleep till tomorrow night. I pass them on to No. 16 at Ecloo."

I turned to the Corporal, thrusting a packet of paper money into his hands. He grasped my hand.

"You're a sport, nurse, you are," he said.

William caught the other hand.

"Lady, you're the right stuff," he puts in. "Feel sort o' guilty, I do, leaving yer. I 'opes yer gets back to yer 'ome all right."

"I'll be all right," I laughed.—"Now follow the man quickly, and I wish you the best of luck."

They disappeared towards the inn and were swallowed up in the gloom. Then, wearily, I waded my way into Lophem, to my aunt's house. An hour later, somewhat dried and refreshed, my aunt summoned me to the back door, and there stood old "Canteen Ma," looking like just a big bundle of clothes, and outside waited her little donkey, harnessed in the little hooded cart. "Canteen Ma" grasped my hand warmly but I said nothing, only crept under the hood, stretched myself among the pots and pans, and fell asleep. My feet burned like red-hot coals and my eyes were shadowed in black, but I was at the hospital at the normal time next morning.

CHAPTER IX

The months went by and I carried on the normal routine of my espionage duties. My weekly reports passed regularly over the counter of the little shop; it was unexciting, and had begun to seem just a normal part of the daily round.

One Saturday evening in May, when I came into the back parlour, I found Fashugel and one of his lieutenants gazing in a depressed fashion on the ground, both their hands thrust deep into their pockets.

"Well, what time to-morrow is this blasted church parade, did you say?" Fashugel was asking, as he irritably kicked the leg of a chair with his boot.

"Ten o'clock—but we'll have to be up long before that. No Sunday sleep for us to-morrow. It is going to take about two hours to march to Westroosebeke. We shall have to parade at seven-thirty at the latest."

Neither of the men took any notice of me and I pretended to be searching for something in my work-basket. Fashugel blew out a cloud of cigar smoke.

"I wish to the devil they would be content on sending the padre round to visit us, instead of collecting the whole division together at some God-forsaken spot to meet the padre——!"

So a whole division would be collected at Westroosebeke at ten o'clock on Sunday morning.

"I suppose you will be wanting your breakfast early to-morrow morning, Herr Hauptmann," I suggested.

"Yes, if you please, Martha—as if we hadn't got enough work to do without having to spend our Sunday mornings tramping about the countryside—well, all I can say is, it will jolly well serve the Divisional Staff right if the 'Seven Sisters' fly over and blow them all to kingdom come——"

"I hope they don't do that," put in the lieutenant with a chuckle, "because after all, you know, as well as blowing up our bloated Staff, who would undoubtedly be the better for it, they might blow us up too."

"What is the idea of a big church parade like that?" I asked. "It seems to me to be dangerous!"

"Oh, there's some big bug of a bishop coming to tell the licentious soldiery how to look after their souls. I expect it will do us all a lot of good, but I wish they would let me stay in bed, all the same."

I took up some sewing and took no further part in the conversation. A whole division was to stand on parade at Westroosebeke at ten o'clock to-morrow morning. They would make a fine mark from the air, for such a large body could not possibly be under cover in my shell-shattered village.

If I passed a warning note immediately, whispering to the grey-haired little chemist in the shop that it was terribly urgent, the message would be over the frontier before dawn on Sunday and from there a code wire could reach the front in ample time for the "Seven Sisters" to pay Westroosebeke a visit. I hoped that Fashugel and several other officers and men with whom I had come in personal contact would not suffer, but this was war and one had to be hard-hearted. I foresaw that the carnage might be ghastly, for the buildings had been practically pounded out of existence, the trees had been blown down or removed for fuel and the landscape was utterly bare.

I supposed the Staff which had arranged the parade considered Westroosebeke a good central gathering spot for the Division, and had thought that by only issuing orders for it late in the day before it was to take place, they would preserve it from the attentions of enemy aircraft. It was one of those still, mellow evenings when all life in the streets seems to go silently, and the fiery red of the setting sun reflected through the chemist's window upon the rows of glass bottles on the shelves as I slipped my note to the polite little chemist, murmuring "To-night," as I did so. I just could not bring myself to realize what a desperate debacle I was trying to bring about, for it all seemed so remote on that beautiful evening.

I was at the hospital at the usual time on Sunday morning, longing for the distant church parade to take place, desperately eager to hear the result, yet afraid. The troops were about to move off. I could hear hoarse commands, and the crash of military boots echoing from the streets far and near, then came the music of the bands, the steady throb of marching feet, and silence fell on half-deserted Roulers. The ward orderly stood beside me.

"The Oberartz would like to see you in the office, sister," he said.

"Fräulein," began the Oberartz, glancing up as I entered. "The Bishop who is taking this big church parade at Westroosebeke has asked that any wounded men at the hospital who are anxious to attend this service and are fit enough to do so should be given every facility to get there. Twelve men have asked to go, and Brigade are sending round a lorry for them presently. Some of them are still lying-down cases—and you never know, they might suddenly take a turn for the worse, or a wound might burst, so I don't think that it will be really wise to only send an orderly with them. I should like you to go with them in the lorry, Fräulein; you have no objection, I suppose."

"None, Herr Oberartz," I answered, closing the door behind me and walking up the passage somewhat dazedly. Gradually the ironic truth began to dawn on me in the full force of its mockery. I had strived to bring about a flaming inferno of agonizing death for others, and now I was to be in it myself, taking my chance against disaster of my own making with those others. At first I felt unutterably frightened, and I confess I could think only of myself. I found myself praying that the "Seven Sisters" would not get my warning in time, for if they did I could see in my mind only too plainly the scene that would ensue; the vast, closely packed, grey masses bursting suddenly like the waters of a dam in every direction as the fierce roar of the "Seven Sisters" eclipsed the clashing of the bands and the singing voices, the crash of bomb upon bomb and the horrible screams, the gathering roar as the relentless planes dived down upon desperate streams of fugitives, machine-gunning them down in helpless, struggling swathes.

Bowling along the road towards Westroosebeke with the lorry full of wounded half an hour later, the kiss of the warm sun stirred my spirits. I looked at the blue sky, wondering in an impersonal way, if this was the last time I should see it. In the background hovered that vague feeling of fear as experienced by someone who is on his way to hospital to undergo a dangerous but inevitable operation. We caught up with the long marching column from Roulers, and as we rumbled past I wondered how many of those men, marching with careless heart behind the blaring bands, were marching to their death.

There was practically nothing left of Westroosebeke—which I had not seen since that morning I had left it with the other women early in 1915—nothing but low walls and piles of broken bricks and fragments. Already large numbers of troops were waiting, formed in close ranks on the outskirts of the village. As the lorry slowed down I could not help thinking of the felon arriving at the place of execution, try as I would. How I hoped that the "Seven Sisters" would not come! And yet, strangely enough, how I wanted them to come!

Soon all the Division had marched on to the ground, and we now formed a dense square, with the Bishop, the officiating padres, the bands and the officers in the middle. The lorry with the twelve wounded was drawn up beside the officers, and the service began. I kept straining my ears for the ominous sound of approaching planes, but nothing broke the sunny stillness but the droning voice from the centre of the square. When the hymns came and it was useless to listen for distant sounds, I gazed fearfully around me, searching for approaching specks on the distant skyline. The service was drawing to a close, the last hymn was announced: disappointment mingled in me with relief. The bands played the opening strains and the chorus of rough voices joined them. Then suddenly in a flash the "Seven Sisters" seemed to be right over us with a mighty roar. It all happened just as I had pictured—the thundering detonations of the bombs, the quivering earth, the showers of rubble and the acrid smoke, shouting men scattering in all directions, the whirring of angry propellers and the rattle of machine-guns as the "Sisters" swooped down so that their wheels almost decapitated the crouching soldiers who ran from them. The Division had faded away, but where it had been was thickly covered with huddled grey forms, battered band instruments and here and there the jagged rent of a bomb crater.

In every direction the whole countryside was dotted with little hastening groups in twos and threes, anxious to put the danger zone behind them. The "Seven Sisters" were zooming overhead in great sweeping circles, every now and then diving with savage bursts of machine-gun fire to encourage the unfortunates below to fresh efforts to escape. It made me think of a day when I had watched police dispersing industrial strikers. They must have had a good laugh, those airmen. As for the twelve wounded and myself, we were ensconced in comparative safety beneath the lorry.

At the first onset we had been as much exposed as anyone else in the open lorry, and bullets were striking all about us, but fortunately there was no casualty. Then the medical orderly had shouted, "Hey, sister—let's get the men underneath the lorry," and with that we set to work. Four of the men could not use their legs and three needed much help, but with the assistance of the remainder, we quickly had them out of the lorry, only the orderly receiving wounds in the forehead and neck. "Knubs" from the nearby ranks had rushed under the lorry for cover, and at first it looked as though they were not going to give way for us. Then a Gefreiter scrambled out from between the wheels shouting, "Come on, you men, give the wounded a chance—they haven't all got sound legs to save themselves with, like you have." and after that they crawled out cheerfully and took their chance in the open.

The "Seven Sisters" soon grew tired of harassing the fugitives, who were becoming more and more widely scattered, and I think also this sort of slaughter appeared too "easy money" to be greatly to their liking. They could certainly feel content with the damage they had done. At a signal from their leader they swerved into formation and sailed away out of sight.

The N.C.O.'s and officers began to collect their men. Wherever I looked I could see still forms lying in the grass. A senior officer came up breathless.

"Sister," he instructed peremptorily, "you will return to Roulers with the lorry immediately. The Oberartz at the hospital is to send every available ambulance, a lorry-load of dressings and as many doctors and dressers as he can spare. The hospital will prepare to receive heavy casualties."

I nodded, and climbed into the lorry. Little did that florid Colonel think that the person he had just despatched for aid was she who was responsible for all the trouble!

Slowly the casualties were brought back to Roulers and I was working at the hospital all the rest of that day and all through the night to make them comfortable. Those well enough were immediately evacuated elsewhere to make room for the others. I refused to let myself think.

Crossing the Place on my way home about eight o'clock the next morning, I noticed "Silent Willy" slouching across to his billet on the opposite side with a pannikin of tea. I was glad he was alive, and that made me think of Fashugel. I went upstairs to my room, and noticed with more than gladness that the door of Fashugel's room stood a quarter open and that there was movement inside. A little later, after washing and tidying myself, I went down to see what food we had in the house. When I was half-way down the stairs, I heard a dull thud of some heavy body on the landing, and glancing up saw that Fashugel's batman had just thrown out a large canvas kit-bag through the door of his room. Then the man himself came out carrying a suitcase. I caught my breath.

"Is the Herr Hauptmann going away?" I put tremulously.

"He's gone, Fräulein," he muttered grimly.

"What do you mean?"

"All we could find of the Herr Hauptmann yesterday morning was a split field-boot with a spur on it. I'm taking his gear along to Brigade now so that it can be sent home to his mother.—It's a pity, for we'll not get another company commander like him if this cursed War lasts till the crack of Doom—yes, a bloody fine officer was our Fashugel, and the fellows will miss him!"

≈

Summer passed uneventfully, and the Germans in Roulers became daily more disillusioned with the War. The newspapers, naturally influenced by German agency, kept stressing the slogan, "Our condition may be BAD, but that of the Allies is far WORSE!"—lavish praise was regularly plastered on "our glorious U-boats," which according to the accounts were so liberally besprinkling the seabed with hostile shipping and through whose efforts ere long the Allies would have to surrender or starve. Notwithstanding this, however, I think the Germans had in their hearts a sneaking distrust of the coming impotence of England, for "God Straffe England" was continuously on German lips, mouthed with virulent fierceness, which sounded like tearful resentment. America just then came in for many sneers and jibes, thanks to the meek and mild policy of President Wilson, and their objections to having their shipping torpedoed and destroyed was regarded by the Germans as being quite outrageously forward for such a retiring nation. Nobody thought the Americans would really come in against Germany.

Towards the autumn, the German General Staff issued orders which had their repercussion behind the lines. One day Alphonse came into my ward and made a signal that he wished to speak to me outside. In the corridor he handed me a buff form, a requisition for medical supplies, and whispered hurriedly:

"This has come from the aerodrome hospital section. You have been waiting to get inside the Rumbeke Aerodrome for a long time. Here is your chance. All these articles requisitioned are small and can be carried in one case. You can call there and leave them with Feldwebel Schweitzer on your way home."

I seized the excuse for entering the aerodrome eagerly and put the requisition in my pocket. Several times during the summer, messages had reached me from over the frontier asking for information about Rumbeke Aerodrome, the enterprising personnel of which had been causing much trouble to the Allies, but had found no excuse to examine it at close quarters, for any unauthorized person prying in its vicinity would have found short shift at the hands of a firing party.

"And here is something special for you," Alphonse went on. "In the Canteen they are talking of the recent successful bombing of London. Mathy, the Zeppelin commander, is being made a hero. They say he is to lead a colossal raid very soon which will cripple the English and create terror and consternation throughout the country."

He broke off and saluted as one of the staff surgeons came round the corner. I walked behind the officer, giving mechanical replies to his routine questioning. Should I be able to learn anything definite about this raid at the aerodrome? Some hope lay in Feldwebel Schweitzer. I had known him well before he had been drafted to the Aerodrome unit as I had had to work with him in the hospital a good deal. He was a rough boor of a man, with the overbearing mannerisms of the old regular army to which he had belonged, but honest enough at heart. He used to stroke his moustaches and make boisterous love to me in odd corners, seeming childishly pained and surprised at the cold reception he had received. However he could not take many liberties with me in hospital corridors, so I had not bothered my head about him overmuch. The medical hut at the Aerodrome was different and I should have to be more careful. Then I must be extremely cautious what I said in the precincts of the Aerodrome where everyone was prone to be suspicious.

There were moments when I was horribly afraid of detection and its consequences. At times lately I had felt that I was watched and suspected, yet some queer impulse drove me on. I was caught up in the wheels of the machine and there was no stopping till some grim mechanic put his hand to the lever. Alphonse was right in what he said, now I came to think about it, not only the troops in the Canteen, but the whole administrative staff who were supposed to really know things, were more noisily optimistic than they had been for months. So this was going to be another case of ending the War, the crushing of the most tenacious and indefatigable foe. And for all I knew this devastating raid might be planned for this week or next.

Feldwebel Schweitzer lay snoring in his bunk. The dispensary was empty, but through the open door I could see his stockinged feet on the end of the stretcher which he had improvised as a bed. At my knock he roused.

"What the hell——?" he growled. "Didn't I give orders that I wasn't to be disturbed—ah. Fräulein—wie reizend.— Thank God for a pretty face! You have brought the medical stores. I thank you, mein Fräulein."

Red-faced, with his coarse shirt unbuttoned to show a hairy chest, he scrambled to his feet, hunting for his boots.

A TYPICAL WAYSIDE SCENE IN OCCUPIED AREAS

HINDENBURG, THE KAISER, AND LUDENDORFF LEAVING HEADQUARTERS

GERMAN LONG-RANGE GUN

A NEWLY ARRIVED BATCH OF BRITISH PRISONERS

BESIDE THE THOROUT ROAD

ROULERS, THE MENIN ROAD

MYSELF TODAY

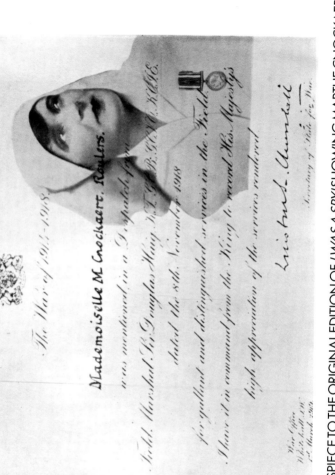

THE FRONTISPIECE TO THE ORIGINAL EDITION OF *I WAS A SPY!* SHOWING MARTHE CNOCKAERT'S CERTIFICATE FROM THE BRITISH WAR OFFICE, SIGNED BY WINSTON CHURCHILL

"Enter, then," he smirked, when he had dressed himself. "This is something of a social occasion. Sit here, so that we cannot be seen and interrupted by others who may also value your company, meine liebe Fräulein."

After poking his head round the corner he shut the door and offered me a cigarette. He had all the air of a mischievous conspirator, and I became rather apprehensive. However, I had got to contrive to make him feel that I had somewhat changed my attitude towards him for the better since our last meeting. For a while we chatted like old and tried friends. Presently he said:

"Soon this filthy War will end. I am sick of this business. Already we are dealing those English a damned hot time. Yes—Mathy knows how to catch them on the hop, by God."

"Who is this Mathy from whom you expect such great things?" I put innocently.

"Mathy, you don't know about Mathy? Well, perhaps you wouldn't hear much about him at the hospital. Mathy is our great Zeppelin leader who is making the complaisant Englanders at home understand what War feels like. That's the way to do them in—attack them at the roots. —Well, they've only had a taste as yet of what is coming to them. You ought to have read the accounts in the German papers of his last few raids. And those were just sort of hors d'œuvres while our Mathy was learning his technique, so to speak. I bet there are quite a lot of people over in England saying their prayers of a night in these days." He chuckled hoarsely. "You're as good as German, mein Fräulein—and prettier than most—so I can speak to you plainly, eh? I have it straight from the batman of the Air Kommandant. Last night the officers feasted on roast hare and sausage, though where the devil they got it from I don't know! Pflugel, the batman, was kept on the run all night, for they were drinking toasts and singing as if they had gone crazy. He helped to carry the Kommandant to bed; and later, when he had him safely tucked beneath the sheets, he got confidential and started to talk about all sorts of things which we poor soldiers aren't expected to know!"

Schweitzer roared with laughter and slapped his leg, and I began to feel afraid that his amusement over the failings of his officers was going to lead him into lengthy reminiscences about them, at the expense of what he had hinted he was about to tell me. But he grew confidential.

"Take it from me," he grinned, "there is going to be no mistake this time. Word has come through from the Higher Command. On the 1st of October—you will see!" He wagged his close-cropped head mysteriously. "It will be the most KOLOSSAL raid of the War, and London will go—pouff." He threw up his hands in a dramatic gesture. "It is said Mathy is to lead eleven Zeppelins," he continued. "Two go from Bruges, the rest from the Fatherland. By Christmas we shall be home, nein?"

He smiled to himself delightedly, showing tobacco-stained teeth. Then his mood changed.

"Come and sit here, don't be so shy," he urged naïvely, patting his bunk. "Come, what about a kiss?"

Suddenly his long arms were around me, his lips slobbering over my face. I tried to wrench myself away, but he had a hug like a bear. For what seemed hours I struggled. Beads of sweat came out on Schweitzer's red face and he panted like an animal. Suddenly he hurled me backward so that my knees caught the edge of the stretcher, and gave a grunt of triumph. I screamed, hardly hoping that anyone would hear, for the medical hut was isolated some little distance from the rest of the buildings, but suddenly the door opened. Over the German's shoulder I saw an officer looking down at us.

"What's all this—what the blasted hell is going on here, Schweitzer?" he shouted in a thunderous voice.

Schweitzer jumped as if shot, and stood regarding the officer in a hang-dog way, like a man dazed.

"Stand to attention when I speak to you, d'you hear? What are you doing with this woman? Why is there nobody on duty?— Great God, you, Fräulein!"

Questions and fury gushed from him, while Schweitzer stood like a ramrod. He was the duty officer for the day at the Aerodrome; and incidentally I knew him; he was one of their crack pilots with a great reputation; not long before he had been badly wounded in an air combat, and had been in the hospital for a month for treatment, where we had become good friends. I explained to him my reason for being at the Aerodrome.

"Well, you have good taste, at any rate, Feldwebel Schweitzer," he said more calmly. "I shall make a report on this and you will be severely dealt with. I am exceedingly sorry that this should have occurred, Fräulein. Follow me, please," and he closed the door behind us, leaving Feldwebel Schweitzer to his thoughts.

"Fräulein," he ventured, "I have not seen you for a long time now. Do me an honour this evening if you are feeling in a gracious mood. Come and dine with me. I am on duty, as you see; so to-night I am destined to dine here at the Aerodrome in the duty officer's hut in solitary state; at least I was so destined until I met you." He turned and caught my hands. "You will be kind—eh, mein Fräulein?"

"Very well, Herr Lieutenant," I smiled, "I will dine with you, but I shall not stay late afterwards."

Indeed, I could not afford to do so, for Schweitzer's tale had had the ring of truth in it, and in any case, I could afford to take no chances. If this gigantic raid was to take place so very soon, the warning must reach London at the earliest possible opportunity for adequate defences to be prepared. The duty officer's hut was at the opposite end of the broad track through the Aerodrome, and as we went I tried to photograph on my mind a detailed picture of the whole place. Suddenly my eye caught five planes drawn up on the edge of the landing ground, and close by a new wooden hangar was in the course of building. These were single-seater biplanes with little fair round bodies suggestive of speed, of a type I had not seen before. I had noticed that the doors of all the hangars were padlocked, which probably meant that the planes they housed were inside, and as the five strange-looking planes had been put to bed for the night in the open, I decided "to put out a cautious feeler."

"I see you are overflowing here, Herr Lieutenant," I said lightly, beckoning towards the row of biplanes.

"Ah, the little Albatrosses, Fräulein—yes, we have not had time to house them yet. They suddenly appeared out of the sky on the evening of the day before yesterday without any previous warning. They are straight from the factory and we are the first to get them.—The Kommandant handed them over to my flight for service testing out.—I have just been writing my report for him about their behaviour in the air, and I can tell you it is a glowing affair!—Splendid little planes, Fräulein—splendid. They climb like rockets, answer to the slightest touch, and what is even better, go a good twenty miles faster than anything the Allies can put in the air.—The damned Englanders have been doing too well up among the clouds of late, but now they are going to sing a new song, I think!"

He had quite obviously had several drinks; but, knowing him of old, I had recognized that from the first. His eyes were muzzy, and he had that tired loping gait and meandering manner of speaking which bespeaks the man who is pleasantly oiled with alcohol. At the hospital he had always said that if it was not for alcohol, he would never have had the courage to leave the ground at all. I determined that that night he should drink as much as I could well encourage him to do.

"Well, Fräulein," he encouraged, throwing open the door of the duty officer's hut. "I can't offer you a first-class dinner, I'm afraid; but it's as good as you would find at home, I expect, in these hard times—and there's plenty to drink at any rate."

Selecting a bottle from the little group which clustered on the central table, he poured two kummels.

"Here's your health, mein Fräulein.—It is not every day in Belgium one is privileged to have a pretty girl at the dinner-table."

He summoned an astonished batman, ordered him to scrape together the best dinner he could possibly manage, and said he didn't care if he stole the food off the Brigadier's table so long as he was quick about it and took care he was not caught. Then we sat and talked while our dinner was preparing. He was as pleased as a boy that he had a lady to dine with him, and during the next half-hour as we sat chatting, I took care he celebrated the event with plenty of kummel. I never asked him a direct question about the Aerodrome, but by casual remarks contrived to set him on the right lines of thought, so that he talked about it spontaneously, and by the time the batman made his reappearance with plates, knives and forks,

I knew how many planes there were in the Aerodrome, their capabilities and much other useful information besides.

The airman rose.

"Fräulein," he said, "will you excuse me for a moment. I have to finish my report on the Albatross this evening, for the Kommandant will want to see it to-morrow morning. It is only a matter of five minutes."

He set to work at a table in the corner fitted up as a writing-table. Lying on the Army blanket which acted for a tablecloth were two squares of foolscap paper. One was the partially written report on the new "Albatrosses," and the other I had learnt in our conversation was his application for a much looked-forward to and overdue leave to the Fatherland, which had been signed by his Kommandant and returned to him that evening. I was thinking idly to myself that if only I could get hold of that aeroplane report it would be of great interest to those over the frontier, but had come to the conclusion that I had better be content with what I had learned already, and the batman had left with a look of self-satisfied pride after depositing a savoury-smelling stew on the table; quite possibly containing the meat of a cat or a dog pilfered from a nearby householder, for such by no means ill-tasting meat was considered a "nice change" in those days; when my host finished his writing and joined me.

"If you remember, Fräulein, please remind me to tell my batman to put those two envelopes in the orderly room post-box," he said as he helped me to the stew.

He had folded up the aeroplane report and also his leave application and placed each in a separate official envelope. I could not understand why he should want to send his leave application away again after leave had been granted, so out of mere curiosity I asked him.

"Well, you see, Fräulein, when we have a leave application granted by our Kommandant, we have to send it to Brigade H.Q. for information and filing. They act as administrative centre for the area, and they naturally must know the whereabouts of every officer, at all times."

He had not licked and stuck down the sticky address label on either of the envelopes, presumably leaving that faintly unpleasing task for his faithful batman, and as we ate an idea occurred to me. The envelope in which he had put his leave application must be addressed to the Brigade Major at H.Q., and the one holding the aeroplane report would be addressed to his Kommandant at the Aerodrome orderly room. The two envelopes were still open. Supposing that I could change over the contents, so that the aeroplane report went to Brigade and vice versa, I believed I might be able to procure a copy of the aeroplane report down to the last detail.

Stephan, the clerk at Brigade, had been made a Gefreiter, and in this capacity was employed as what was known as confidential clerk to the Brigade Major, as such incidentally having handed me much useful information in the past. One of his duties was to open and place in appropriate piles for the Brigade Major's inspection, all official correspondence which was not marked SECRET, and naturally an envelope bearing a supposed leave application would not fall into this category. Now a report on the flying abilities of a new type of aeroplane was no use to Brigade, was not wanted by Brigade, and would be of no more interest to an overworked Brigade Major than a report on the birth-rate in the Congo. I felt quite sure that if Stephan were to say upon opening it, "Here is some sort of report on an aeroplane, Herr Major, addressed to the Aerodrome Kommandant, which must have been sent here by mistake," that the rejoinder would be: "Oh, push it in an envelope, and send it along to the Kommandant with a covering slip explaining we received it in error," and that after that the great man would forget all about it and Stephan would be able to copy and return it at his leisure. If I could only effect the change and warn Stephan, the affair would be simple.

Fortunately my friend helped me himself in this matter. When we had finished eating he discovered that his batman had forgotten to bring across his brandy with his drinks from his billet which was not far distant, and he rushed to the door and angrily throwing it open, stood outside and started to roar for him lustily. And here the good batman helped me also, for he was chatting with the men in the guard-room some distance away and did not hear his master for some time. I made the change like lightning, though my fingers seemed to fumble maddeningly, and I was terrified that he might turn to speak to me through the door. When he returned grumbling at his batman, I was back in my place. A few minutes later, at his master's order (I had to remind him), the batman had stuck up the envelopes and removed them.

But that evening was not quite over for me. In politeness to my host, I felt bound to stay for a short time. My host had certainly imbibed a great deal by this time. He started by being heroic and telling me about his adventures and exploits, and all the notches he had carved on his joy-stick, then he became maudlin in an amorous way. Unexpectedly, he pushed his chair back with a mischievous expression on his face, took a key from his pocket and wandered over and locked the door.

"Now nobody can come and interrupt us," he informed me slyly.

He fumbled for his pocket to replace the key, but to my inexpressible relief I saw it drop on to the floor. He did not notice this, however, as a new idea had entered his head and was occupying his mind. He drew himself up with a magnificent gesture, and wallowed across to the table with solemn mien.

"I drink to BEAUTY," he announced triumphantly, trying to pour two glasses of brandy into one wine-glass, and raising it on high where most of the liquid upset down his sleeve. He came round slowly to the back of my chair. His hand slipped round my neck, while his lips touched my hair, sending a cold wave through me. His eager face was bent so close over mine that I could see the little hairs on his cheeks above the shaven line. I jumped up and poured myself a drink.

"I think you are altogether too impatient," I told him lightly. "Perhaps you have forgotten, but you were telling me all about yourself when you interrupted your story to behave in this silly way. I was interested, so why don't you tell me some more——?"

He thumped down with sprawled legs and a foolish grin on the seat I had just vacated, and sat opposite.

"Well, well, meine liebe Fräulein, I am sorry, but you are worth being impatient about, you see."

Then he began about himself again. He knew he was a very brave man, and short of actually telling me as much, did his best to prove it in a welter of irrelevant anecdotes and repetitions. One thing I did listen to carefully, however, and it was certainly more than I was expecting, and that was that on the Friday of that week he was to lead the light fighters which were to escort the heavy bombers on a night-raid against Poperinghe, the key to the whole British line, the great railhead of the sector. With the usual German optimism he announced that the place was to be bombed out of existence. At last he stopped talking and rose somewhat shakily with that mischievous look coming back to his face again.

"Fräulein—I want a reward for saving you from the clutches of that baboon Schweitzer. Kiss me"—and he blundered towards me.

Like a flash I was at the door, had seized the key, and was through, locking it on the outside. When he banged on the door, I said:

"Sorry, Herr Lieutenant, you will have to go on being patient. Don't drop the key on the floor next time you dine with one of your lady friends——."

"Open that door," he roared like an angry child.

"Now, if you aren't good, Herr Lieutenant," I admonished, "I shall leave you locked in your room and give the key to the sentry, telling him how bad you've been.—And that would be a terribly undignified position for a duty officer of the day to find himself in. Now—will you let me go quietly and be good if I let you out?"

There was a pause, then a sulky voice muttered:

"Oh, all right, Fräulein, I'll do as you say. Open the door."

It sounded as if the little incident had sobered him up a little. He came out on to the step looking very angry. I took hold of his hand, saying,

"Well, thank you ever so much for asking me to dine with you, Herr Lieutenant. I've had a lovely evening. Good night."

In spite of himself he could not help smiling.

"You little devil," he murmured. "You've certainly made a nice fool out of me——"

"Don't be silly, you've made a fool out of yourself," I sent back over my shoulder.

"You are right, Fräulein, and I'm sorry. Forgive me, please," was the reply.

"Of course," I told him. "Good night once again, and perhaps I shall see you again some time." I passed the sentry without question, for no doubt he had heard all about the duty officer's lady visitor from his batman.

I decided to call at the chemist's shop immediately, where I could code a message about the Zeppelin raid on London, and the bombing of Poperinghe, for there was no time to be lost. The street was utterly deserted, and I had just rapped hard on the door when a figure appeared out from the shadow of the houses and halted before me. It was a gendarme.

"May I see your pass, sister," he drawled. "I see this gives you permission to go to and from the hospital at any time during curfew hours. There is no mention that you may visit private houses that I can see here."

My head swam. Then I retorted:

"It's really quite simple, Corporal. My father suffers from the earache very badly—he is an old man, you know, and to-night a painful attack has come on. I came to the chemist to buy some glycerine."

He handed me back my pass.

"That will be all right, sister," he said; "good night," and continued on his way.

I found an excuse to speak with Alphonse as soon as I arrived at the hospital the next morning, and instructed him to get in touch with Stephan over the aeroplane report. That same afternoon Stephan brought the copy he had made round to the back entrance of the café and left it with my mother. It was too large to hand over the counter at the chemist's with any degree of safety, so I had to invent another method of transmission. The report covered three pages of foolscap, and I cut them into thin strips which I numbered so that they could be easily reassembled in the proper order. These I sewed into the hem of an old skirt, and when "Canteen Ma" called the following morning with vegetables, my mother ostensibly presented her with an old skirt for herself.

On the night scheduled for the bombing of Poperinghe, the British made a counter-raid on Rumbeke Aerodrome, with the idea, I suppose, of killing the German effort before it was born. But the British arrived a trifle too late. They met the German raiders already on their way and passing over Roulers. A furious combat opened above us. The German gunners on the ground could not fire for fear of hitting their own people, and orders were given that the searchlights should cease to play into the sky, for their beams obviously helped friend as much as foe. A British plane descended in flames and trailing smoke. Then another British plane and a German plane spun flaming to the ground simultaneously—a collision. The German was my friend of the Aerodrome, and he was dead when they found him. In the darkness the Germans succeeded in giving the slip to the British and continued on their way towards Poperinghe. The town was ready, and guided by the searchlights, the defensive barrage immediately crashed into life. One German plane fell, and after dropping a few bombs which did no serious damage, the others vanished. This was what I heard from "Canteen Ma," who had it from over the frontier.

At last the evening of the 1st October, the appointed time for the Zeppelin raid, arrived. For days I had wondered whether perhaps it had been a mere canard, a soldier rumour. But at five in the evening of October 1st, I heard the drone of Zeppelin engines. It was almost dark, with low clouds, but there was no mistaking that sinister sound. Whether there were one or two, I did not know, but plainly my information had been correct. Maybe the famous Mathy was in that machine going to rendezvous on the unlit English coast, ready to rain death and ruin on helpless non-combatants. I did not know whether I should ever hear the result of that grim night's work, but as I stared up into the darkening sky, I prayed that for Mathy and his companions it would be a failure.

I was fated not to hear what took place when the raiders came over London on that memorable night till years later, after the Armistice. Meanwhile Mathy had gone to his doom. It is a matter of history how well prepared the defences of London were, and how Lieutenant Tempest shot down the L31 over Potter's Bar till it crumpled into a blazing ruin. Such was the end of a brave man and one of the foremost of German Air Commanders.

CHAPTER X

During the first week in October "Canteen Ma" failed to call for the first time since I had been associated with her; nor did she come the following week. Stephan told me that at the canteen they were buying their fruit from a new source. Another week passed, then my mother told me that the driver of the contractor's dray that brought our supplies of liquor to the café was asking to see me. He was standing just inside the back door when I came down.

"Good evening, Mademoiselle," he began in a gruff voice. "Here are the goods waiting outside. Will you check the voucher, please." As I took the voucher I was aware that with it he had placed in my hands a small paper cylinder, and I looked up startled. He said nothing, but raised his coat lapel and I saw two diagonally placed safety-pins.

"What has happened to "Canteen Ma?" I put as I handed back the voucher.

"I don't know, but I suppose her luck deserted her. I doubt if you'll ever buy any fruit from her again. At any rate, I am in future to be the receiver of the instructions that are to be carried out by you." He touched his cap and was gone. So I should see poor, cheerful old "Canteen Ma" with her creaking cart no more. Perhaps she had already faced a firing squad in the dawn.

About the end of October the Germans began to accumulate a large dump of supplies and rifle ammunition in the grounds of a house near the centre of the town. By that time the Allies had lost the supremacy in the air owing to the production of the fast German "fighter" of the Albatross and similar types, and as the vicinity of the dump was strongly defended with anti-aircraft guns, I thought it unlikely that a successful raid could be conducted on this dump. I still had the two sticks of dynamite which I had taken from the pocket of Edmund No. 8, and the thought occurred to me that some use might be made of these if only the ring of sentries which patrolled the outside of the walls around the grounds could be penetrated. The explosion of two dynamite sticks among the stores would quickly turn the whole place into a raging furnace. I told Alphonse of my idea, but he shook his head and said it was madness, for it would be quite impossible to evade the sentries. Several evenings afterwards, however, I found Alphonse awaiting me in the backparlour. There was an eager look in his face, so that involuntarily I asked, "What is it?"

"I have had a brain wave," he said. "It is over this question of the stores dump in the town.—To do what I am thinking about would certainly be a great risk, and into the bargain it might turn out a failure in the end—but then, of course, it might not!—And in that case it would give the Germans something to rack their brains about for several weeks afterwards." He sat down and lit a cigarette. "Yes—it is without doubt an *idea* that I have in mind, Martha," he mused, with a thoughtful smile on his face.

"Tell me, please, Alphonse," I begged.

"Well, it is this way.—In 1914 a good many shells landed in the vicinity of Roulers, and one of them left a crater in the hospital grounds. But there was something more than just a crater there. At the bottom of that crater there was a round black hole which had apparently been pierced through stonework. It looked as if the shell had unearthed an old secret passage and several of us went down with torches. It seemed to lead for miles and miles under the town, but to get nowhere in particular."

"I don't remember ever having heard anybody mention such a place at the hospital," I put in.

"No—because I think everybody has forgotten about its existence. The men who explored the place with me have all been transferred to other units, and besides not long afterwards the present wooden staff hut was built over the spot."

"Exactly what is it you have in mind that we should do?"

"To continue my story, Martha—I had always been interested in antiquities, and my historical sense was intrigued over that passage and the reasons for it being made. In a second-hand book-shop I found an old history of Roulers. I learnt that at one time, as in so many medieval towns, an open sewer ran through the middle of the main street and crossed the fields to the river, and I came to the conclusion that what we had taken to be a secret passage was really this sewer. Having found out that much, I was satisfied, and forgot that the sewer existed——"

"You mean that we might in some way use this sewer to gain an entrance to the grounds where the stores are?"

"Yes—I first thought of it one night when I came across the old book in my kit, although at first it was just idle speculation. But there was a town plan in the front of the history, and working things out by the church, the beginnings of the Grand Place and several other landmarks which still exist, I formed the conclusion that the main thoroughfare of that time, with the sewer, passed across ground where the dump is now located.—If we could make our way along the sewer until we are beneath the dump, we might 'come to ground' within the ring of sentries, do our work and vanish, leaving it to burn to its heart's content——"

"That sounds splendid, but suppose we misjudge the distance we have to go along the sewer and stick our heads out of the ground after curfew hour in the middle of the Grand Place or even at the feet of one of the sentries——"

"Well, Martha, I told you that there was a risk, and that is where that risk comes in!" said Alphonse with a shrug. "You are perfectly right, it is possible even that we might appear through the floor of the Town-Kommandant's office, but if we are careful and use our common sense I don't think we should do so.—Up to a point it is possible to make calculations. Throughout its course the sewer runs straight, and measuring on a large scale-map of the town and district which was hanging in the hospital, I have estimated that from the hospital to a point in Roulers which would roughly mark the centre of the grounds where the dump has been collected, is a distance of three kilometres."

"It is not going to be so easy to calculate how far along the sewer you have gone underground."

Alphonse lit another cigarette and flicked the burnt match with a fine gesture into the fire. "I had even thought about that, Martha, and it is fairly simple, really—I have a length of string 100 metres long, to each end of which I have tied a small peg. There are 3000 metres in 3 kilometres, which is the distance we have to cover, and therefore thirty times the length of my string would bring me 3000 metres from my starting-point, in other words to the spot where I wished to come up in the centre of the dump.—Now, let us suppose you do agree to help me in this, Martha, then upon descending into the sewer at the hospital we shall proceed in this way: you will hold the peg at one end of the string and I grasping the other peg shall walk along the sewer until the string is stretched taut between us, signifying that I have covered 100 metres. I shall then remain stationary and you will pass me and continue until the string is again taut. After repeating this rather tedious process thirty times we shall find ourselves as near to being beneath the centre of the dump as we can ever hope to be." Alphonse finished his second cigarette in silence. "Well, Martha," he demanded at last, "what do you say?"

"We'll have a try at it," I decided. "When do you suggest we start, as it looks as if this little job is going to occupy a night or two?"

"To-morrow night seems to me to be as good as any, provided I don't get sent up the front with my ambulance. Find an excuse to work late at the hospital, and at nine o'clock meet me at the right end of the civilians' hut.—I can tell you, Martha, we are going to have an evening of hard toil!"

The following evening I slipped out of the back entrance of the hospital as the distant church clock struck nine, and made my way to the civilians' hut. Except for those who were on duty in the wards, the hospital was generally deserted at that hour. A dim figure was waiting at the right end of the long wooden hut.

"Alphonse?" I ventured in a nervous whisper.

"Good evening, Martha, you are on time. Sit down for a minute and we will talk."

"Well?"

"Since seeing you last night I did some reconnoitring and there are certain things which combine to help us. —As you know, this hut is raised off the ground so as to avoid the damp and rats. Well—this end, owing to the downward slope of the ground, leaves sufficient space under the flooring for us to crawl beneath and slip into the hole, which is better than having to raise half a dozen floor-boards and replace them when we get out. The second piece of good fortune is, that when the workmen had completed their job they found that they had about a dozen good stout boards to spare, and to save carrying them away pushed them underneath the hut."

I inquired what was in the half-filled sack which lay beside him.

"Cement, a padded hammer, a saw, a strong chisel, a mortar and plenty of long nails. I'll not be able to visit the canteen for at least a month, for all my pay is pledged to various shopkeepers in the town for these blasted things," came the impressive reply.

Alphonse stood up and beckoning me to follow, went to the door of the hut, and producing a key from his pocket, led me into the dark interior.

"First," he said, dropping his sack on the floor, "we have got to cover all the windows facing towards the hospital with newspapers to hide our light." He took from the sack some newspapers, and by means of drawing-pins, we covered the windows as best we could in the dark. "For to-night we shall have to raise two of the floor-boards in the right half of the hut," Alphonse explained, "because we have got to get those loose planks of the workmen down into the sewer, and the only way to do that is to lift them upright and drop them perpendicularly down into the hole. They can then be manipulated until we have them lying flat inside the sewer."

After a hard quarter of an hour's work with the tools we had the two narrow sections of boarding removed. Below, near the middle of the hut, the light of the lantern showed part of a gap in the ground, and nearer the end of the hut lay the loose plank.

"How deep is the shaft?" I asked, as we collected the planks before inserting them in the gap.

"Altogether about 2¾ metres [*circa* 9 ft.], the sewer itself is about 2 metres. This is going to be something of a messy job. I hope that cloak of yours is an old one, Martha."

"Wriggling oneself down that hole underneath is likely to be rather a tricky business," I remarked; "and once we are down I don't see how we are ever going to get out again."

"I will scrape away the earth underneath the boards so that it shelves down to the hole. Then if you go feet first, it won't be so bad. As for climbing out, that is one of the occasions in which the planks are coming in useful——"

As one end of the planks was sticking up through the floor and we could not replace the floor-boards until we had pulled those into the sewer, which necessitated climbing down ourselves, we extinguished the light and went outside to the right end of the hut. There was no moon to be seen that night and I was glad! Dragging the sack with him Alphonse crept beneath, and then I heard him scraping away the ground with some metal instrument and the faint rustle of showering earth and pebbles. There was a sound of scrambling, followed by silence. Peering below, I saw the gleam of a light from the depths, and a hollow voice in the distance boomed.

"Well, Martha, I'm down in the sewer, and my mouth is full of dirt; remember to keep yours shut tightly."

Drawing my cloak tightly around me, I edged under the floor feet first, keeping my head well down to prevent bruises.

My feet were over space and I wriggled my legs into the hole pressing my face into the ground. Alphonse caught my waist and a few moments later I was standing on the loose rubble in the musty sewer.

At each side of us yawned a black passageway with walls and ceiling paved with large flat stones. We were shut away from the world in cold, damp stillness. After rummaging in his sack, Alphonse produced the two pegs and the cord.

"We may as well be moving," he muttered, turning up the collar of his greatcoat, and with that handed me a peg and set off into the darkness, holding the other peg in one hand and the lantern in the other. I stood watching the disk of light from the lantern travelling along the roof and listening to the faint hissing of the cord unwinding along the ground. I turned my head for an instant and a thick mesh of cobwebs brushed my forehead, making me shiver. The dust-impregnated atmosphere caught in the throat and nostrils.

I felt a sharp jerk on my peg. The distant ball of light had ceased moving and the cord stretched taut. The voice of Alphonse rolled eerily down the tunnel towards me. I had switched my torch upon the floor ahead and had started to move forward when there came a fierce and prolonged rustling in the opening above. I stopped, frozen with terror. I thought I detected quick breathing. I knew that something was looking down at me, but all was as quiet as the grave. When I flashed my torch upwards two black, beady eyes met mine. Peering down the mouth of the crater was the sleek head of a black rat. Alphonse laughed when I told him, saying he had seen numbers of them scuttling away as he advanced with the light. It was the same throughout the whole of that dismal hour of subterranean walking—one heard nothing but the ever-fleeing rats.

At last the cord had been stretched to its length for the thirtieth time, and copying Alphonse, I sat down beside the lantern and contemplated the stone slab above our heads, of about 65 centimetres square [¾ sq. yard.].

"That slab has got to come out," pronounced Alphonse, handing me a cigarette and lighting it, after which he scraped up a little mound of dirt with his hands to mark the spot and rising on tiptoe drew a cross with white chalk on the doomed stone.

"The whole roof about here may fall in on top of us when we pull away that stone," I suggested.

"Well, I'm not a miner, Martha, but I was brought up in a district of miners. Do you know what a miner would do if he had to remove that stone and he wanted to preserve an unbroken head?—He would put props against the surrounding portions of roof before he started to pick at the mortar to loosen it."

"So that's where those planks are coming in useful?"

"Exactly; that is to say, when we have taken the measurements and cut them to the correct length. We shall also need some kind of ladder to help us to get out both at this end and at the other, and there are several things besides. Consequently we are going to spend the whole of to-morrow evening at carpentry, in this delightful old-world sewer, if you are agreeable, Martha!"

When his cigarette was finished he suggested that by the time we had returned to starting-point, pulled all the planks from the hole down into the sewer, manufactured a rough stepladder to help us out, after the manner of the grooved run into a fowl-house, and replaced the two boards in the civilians' hut, it would be time to knock off work until nine o'clock on the following evening. It was absolutely essential that he should be in his barrack-room by midnight each night, as otherwise he could be crimed as absent without leave; which might lead to awkward questions.

We were standing at the end of the staff hut the next evening discussing our plans before we made our way into the sewer when suddenly Alphonse seized me in his arms, kissing me passionately! I was too amazed to resist, at first— Alphonse the one-time theological student, was the last man I had expected to act in this way—but then the sound of footfalls on the turf close behind us reached me. Three soldiers passed walking in the direction of the hospital. They must have taken a short cut across the grounds. I heard them chuckling among themselves as they disappeared in the darkness.—So the Fräulein at the hospital had a soldier lover!—I did not think that they would be able to see that it was Alphonse.

"That just shows how careful we've got to be, Martha," he said. Then he added, perhaps a trifle sadly: "Do you know, Martha, that quite unforeseen, to-night has made itself into an epoch in my life. For the kiss which I gave you to-night is the last kiss I shall ever give a woman. As soon as this War is over I shall become a priest."

We made our way below in silence. Here we sawed the planks to the right length to make four strong props, our manœuvres being watched by several curious rats, who hastily disappeared when we flashed the light on them. We also made a second rough step-ladder, to be used at the dump opening, like the one we had made to climb out by the night before. Finally, Alphonse nailed together a kind of wooden lid, which puzzled me somewhat. Then he sat down and drew a rough diagram, explaining what he proposed to do.

The wooden lid was for the purpose of camouflaging the hole after the hoped-for explosions and fire took place. The remains of the burnt dump were bound to be salvaged by the Germans, and if they were to come upon a gaping hole in the ground leading to an unsuspected passageway which possessed a further opening at the hospital their suspicions would be pointed in the right direction. The lid was to be covered with a layer of wet cement and earth.

When the slab in the roof was removed the earth above would fall in with a little coaxing from below, and as this would almost certainly drop, leaving a bigger opening at the ground level than the actual size of the slab aperture through which it fell, the lid had to be formed so as to conceal this larger hole, and at the same time to be capable of being passed up complete from the sewer. The wooden lid therefore was longer than the slab, but slightly narrower, so that it could pass through the opening, the deficiency in width being made up for by a fringe of sacking along each side covered with glue and earth, which could be stretched laterally with pieces of wire when the contrivance had been raised from the sewer. While the fuses were being lighted the camouflage lid would be lifted at one end by a prop—as in the diagram(*see* next page)—but as soon as this was cut away it would fall flat with the ground, where it could be walked over without danger of giving way, and was unlikely to attract any but the closest observer.

Having completed our work, we decided that we would spend the next evening in carrying the manufactured articles to beneath the dump, and fitting in position the four roof props—an affair of several journeys. On the evening after that I should bring the dynamite sticks with me and we would make the great attempt. We calculated that the two explosions would occur about 10.30 p.m., as until that time we should be occupied in unpicking the slab, laying the bombs and fuses and fixing the lid.

ALPHONSE'S DIAGRAM

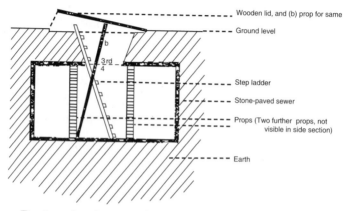

Wooden lid, and (b) prop for same

Ground level

b

3rd/4

Step ladder

Stone-paved sewer

Props (Two further props, not visible in side section)

Earth

During the day on which we were to make our attempt a question was uppermost in my mind which had hardly worried me at all before.—Suppose that we did not emerge from the sewer in the centre of the dump, but that instead we burrowed our way from the ground to find a sentry leaning on his rifle and watching us?—The thought became a positive fear, as, having returned to the café for the dynamite, I was making my way towards the hut by cutting across the hospital grounds. The moon reminded me that it would make things all the easier for a watcher.

When I met Alphonse we hardly addressed a word to each other, but crept into the sewer and hurried through the shadows preceded by our vanguard of frightened rats. Arrived under the stone with the white cross around where we had placed the four props on the previous night, Alphonse and I set to work, gingerly picking away the mortar holding the slab with pickaxes of which we had cut the handles short. We placed a temporary prop up against the stone while we were loosening it, so that it should not unexpectedly crash on our heads. Dust and dirt poured into our upturned faces, half-blinding us; the unusual position made my arms and neck and shoulders a burning agony; the perspiration trickled down my back. Half an hour had passed and all the mortar appeared to have gone from around the marked slab. Alphonse said, "Stand well back, Martha,"— and removed the prop. The slab remained in position.

Taking a small crowbar from his sack, he attacked the open cracks with vigour. The slab began to move, and I thought to myself that our fate might be mixed up with the events of the next few minutes. Alphonse leaped back, and down crashed the slab, sending a thunderous echo resounding through the bowels of the earth. An avalanche of earth and stones roared the echo out of existence, then there was an utter silence. For a moment we stood breathless, as if waiting for something to happen, then I peered upward to see through a ring in the yawning earth a pale radiance which must be the moonlight. Much of the earth overhead had clung together, but after a little work with the crowbar a wide gap lay open above us. We placed the ladder in position silently. Alphonse ascended, and barely raising his eyes above the ground, gazed about.

"Martha, our luck is in. We have struck a good position!" the whisper reached me.

Then he disappeared over the top. A few minutes later his face appeared at the gap.

"Hand up the camouflaged lid, Martha," he hissed. "Then come yourself with the dynamite. We are everywhere protected from the sentries by piles of stores."

On my knees in the open I surveyed my surroundings. The hole was in the shadow of a great stack of tools, and in every direction was a billowing sea of tarpaulin-covered mounds.

"Stay here, I am going to reconnoitre for a good spot to place the bombs," warned Alphonse, and vanished among impediments of the dump. Several times I could hear the measured pacing of the sentries as they passed close to us on their beats. Climbing up on to a pile of casks, I could see here and there the glint off a moving bayonet, and below me, perhaps one hundred yards distant, two shadowy casqued figures met, exchanged a few words, and retired on their beats. A gentle breeze was blowing, sufficient to fan the flames from one pile to another.

There was a sound of scraping behind me and I started, but it was only Alphonse who had joined me.

"Look to your right, Martha," he ordered. "Do you see that dump with a hump-back in the middle, two places away. It consists of tins of petrol. Go and wedge one of the dynamite sticks among the tins, and lead the fuse to our hole.—Give me the other stick. I am going to put it in that big stack of rifle ammunition boxes in the rear."

Keeping in the cover of the other stacks, I slipped towards my objective. I was reaching to lift the tarpaulin when my foot struck a stray petrol tin on the ground which emitted a dull tonk, at the same time grating against the tins at the foot of the stack. It sounded to me like the crack of doom. After a minute's pause a gruff voice not far distant challenged. I shrunk petrified against the stack. The voice challenged again. Hearing no sound the man apparently concluded that the noise could have been nothing of importance, for he made no further investigations. I let two minutes go by without making any move, then, feeling my way with great caution, I raised the tarpaulin and pushed the stick between two tins.

I found Alphonse waiting by the hole. He told me that he had not heard a sound, so the noise I had made could not have been so great after all. We fixed the camouflaged lid at an angle with the prop to facilitate a hasty exit from the upper world, and then we were ready. Alphonse drew the ends of the two fuses together, chuckling: "Well, well, it strikes me that somebody is going to feel surprised in a few minutes.—What a devil of a shame it is we can't watch those sentries hop."

He took a box of matches from his pocket, and I stood behind him, looking round anxiously as he struck a match and shielded the flame with his hand.

"Now, Martha, down into the sewer with you," came the command, "and as soon as my head comes below the parapet knock away the prop—but not before, mind, for I don't want a bump on the head."

I saw him bend and touch the flame to the fuses as my eyes were on a level with the ground, then I heard the fierce fizzling. He paused for a moment to see that they were burning properly, and putting his feet on the rough ladder descended slowly as if he was afraid to leave the fate of his precious scheme at the mercy of the fuses. I struck the prop sharply with a crowbar and the lid fell with a dull thud. It seemed as though we were safe in another world, miles beneath the earth, but I was soon awakened from that dream. Grasping the lantern and the sack and catching my wrist, Alphonse breathed:

"Come, Martha, run, the concussion may possibly bring down some of the roof in this part of the sewer."

We had not gone far when a loud rumbling reverberated after us, followed by a second outbreak which seemed to swallow the first. Involuntarily our hands went up to shield our heads, for everything was rocking about us. Nothing fell, but we had had enough of the sewer, and hastened without a word towards the place of egress at the hospital.

When we emerged from beneath the hut our eyes at once turned in the direction of Roulers. A great yellow glow coloured the darkness over the town.

"I hope everything is destroyed and that they manage to put the fire out," exclaimed Alphonse cheerfully. "I shall have to go to my barrack-room," he went on with a sigh; "but you are more lucky, Martha. You will be able to see some of the fun in Roulers on your way home. Good night, Martha—and many thanks."

He slipped away, and hearing voices which came from a little group of men gathered outside the hospital evidently attracted by the unusual brilliance of the town, I pulled my dark cloak closely around me, and taking off my white coif, set off across the grounds where I was unlikely to be seen. Once the hospital area was behind me I was safe, for I could always say in Roulers that I had been on late duty at the hospital.

When I reached the Grand Place it was almost as bright as day, for away beyond the buildings on the opposite side the flames were leaping high, spitting fountains of crackling sparks into the air. There was a continual din of shouting mingled with the popping of exploding rifle cartridges. The whole garrison of Roulers had been turned out to quell the fire, men were running to and fro, and leaky hose-pipes twined their way across the Place. Not a civilian was in the streets, of course, for they dared not disobey the curfew regulations, but many a curious head peered from the dark windows.

Presently I joined my mother in her room, for the windows faced towards the conflagration. She was watching by the open sill.

"What has happened?" I asked.

"I don't know, Martha, how it started, but suddenly about half-past ten we heard two explosions, then we saw that the big supply dump was on fire. I think that someone in Roulers, who is not a German, could tell an interesting story about this," she opined with a laugh. "But I hope he has not been caught."

"Your hope has been granted, mother," I told her. "The person who did it, or rather took a half-share, is going to sit down and enjoy the sight quite as much as Nero enjoyed the burning of Rome. Only I think perhaps it would be as well if I don't play any musical instrument with this window open, because it might annoy the men who are trying to put out the fire quite a lot."

"I am proud, Martha. But sometimes I feel that one day your luck will leave you," she said, after a little silence.

Towards the morning the fire died down, leaving the dump a mass of charred rubbish which smoked and smouldered throughout the whole of the day. I made a disquieting discovery that morning. My gold wrist-watch was missing. I could not remember the last time I had seen it on my wrist. The clasp of the band had been loose for several days, and I had meant to have it mended but kept postponing this from day to day. It might have dropped off in the hospital before we attempted last night's attempt, it might be somewhere in the tunnel, under the hut, on the site of the wrecked dump, or safer, from my point of view, in the hospital grounds. It was certainly disturbing, for it meant that somewhere there might perhaps exist a piece of evidence which, if found, would cause some very embarrassing questions to be put to me. But I could do nothing, except hope for the best.

The Oberartz sent for me a week later. He had a somewhat grave look on his face, and I felt frightened as I had sometimes done before when I thought there were some possible grounds for suspicion against me. But what he said to me had an entirely different bearing on my future. A matron and a number of German nurses had at last been detailed to the hospital. The Oberartz assured me that he wished me to carry on with my work as before, but added that he thought I might find it hard to work with them and be friendly, and that he and the other surgeons would be always ready to help me and he sincerely hoped that if I cared to remain at my work all would go well.

I had got to remain at the hospital, for my espionage work would become far more difficult if I had to leave. Besides I had grown genuinely attached to my nursing duties and the men who were around me. Eight nurses and a matron duly arrived. Apart from the matron they were young volunteers with little training and no experience. At times they were more nuisance than they were worth, and I think they realized that themselves, for unconsciously the surgeons and orderlies often behaved towards them in an abrupt and impatient manner.

I became the victim of what I am sure was jealousy rather than any outbreak of national indignation. My manner with the patients was confident through long practice, which theirs was not; I was treated with respect. The matron disliked me instinctively, because she and I were just the types of women who invariably do dislike each other. She was thin and bony, with spectacles, and a disappointed look about her. After three days she came up and told me that I talked a great deal too much with the men, but I did not take her very seriously.

Once or twice we should have had furious arguments if I had not given way. At first the younger nurses treated me with condescension, but I tried to be friendly and not to notice it. When they realized that as far as the male staff and the wounded were concerned they were at a discount, the result was inevitable. They refused to speak to me at all, avoided me whenever they could, and when anything had gone wrong which could by any means be blamed on my shoulders tales were told to the doctors behind my back.

At the end of a week the Oberartz summoned me. The matron had reported to him that I was far too friendly with three wounded prisoners. She had also suggested that I should not be permitted to talk to German troops except when this was absolutely necessary in dressing their wounds. The Oberartz had talked her out of such extreme measures, but he urged upon me to be more discreet. A few days later, Alphonse beckoned me aside to tell me that he had overheard some of the sisters discussing me in shrill voices in the dispensary. One of them was recounting that Matron told her that if the Oberartz refused to dismiss me she intended to make a complaint to the Town-Kommandant. This might not have the result she desired, but it was bound to centre the interest of the local authorities temporarily upon me. Awkward questions might be put to me, and the very last thing a spy desires is to be the centre of interest.

Alphonse advised me to leave of my own free will. It would be a handicap to my activities to lose my present privileges, but I was on good terms with many Germans in the town by then and he believed I could carry on well enough on those lines. I decided to do as he said. Alphonse also told me of the findings of the Court of Enquiry over the destruction of the dump, which he had heard about from Stephan. The authorities were utterly nonplussed. None of the sentries had been injured by the explosions and they had all been found at their posts. Not a man had anything to report. The orderly officer who had visited them that night, incidentally not long before the explosions, gave it in evidence that in his opinion the sentries were posted in such a way that it was impossible for a person to pass through them unseen, especially on a moonlit night. They were forced to conclude, somewhat incredulously, that explosive had been accidentally packed among the stocks in the dump and that for some reason unknown it had exploded.

When it became known that I was leaving the hospital everybody except the new nurses was exceedingly nice to me. The Oberartz thanked me for all I had done almost with tears in his eyes. His position was a difficult one; for, although I knew he sympathized with me, he had to stand by his own countrywomen. I promised that if at any time the hospital staff was overworked and extra assistance was needed I would come back. Then I went round the wards saying good-bye to the doctors and all the men I had known. Farewells are always an unpleasant business, and the matter having gone so far, I felt relieved when I had shaken hands with the man at the gates and was walking down the road towards Roulers for the last time. I should still know what was going on in the hospital to some extent, for Alphonse was to come to see me one evening a week.

It was the end of November, and one afternoon I was passing the Town-Kommandant's office in the Place when I happened to glance at the big notice-board by the door, where orders and regulations for the civilians were pinned. One caught my eye:

LOST PROPERTY.

A soldier of the Army of Würtemberg has been apprehended by the military police for theft. A number of articles found in his possession, from their character appear to belong to civilians of the town. Will any person thinking he recognizes any of the following articles please report at this office between the hours of 10 a.m. and 12 noon.——

Fourth on the list which appeared below I read: *A gold wristlet watch with the initials M.C. engraved inside the cover at the back.*

That was almost certainly my watch. Presumably either the thief himself had picked it up, or he had stolen it from some civilian who had done so. At all events, it seemed to clear me. I was anxious to get the little watch back, for it had a sentimental value for me. If only I had thought of that early warning of Lucelle: "and if you are caught it will probably be your own fault," I might have given the matter more thought before I made any move.

I called at the office next morning at 10 o'clock. I knew the Town-Kommandant well and he wished me a smiling "Good morning." When I explained my business he looked rather taken aback, and then muttered: "Oh, yes, would this happen to be yours Mademoiselle Cnockaert?" taking an envelope from an empty drawer and tipping my wrist-watch out upon his desk. I wonder now that the fact it was not among a pile of other articles did not strike me at the time.

"Well, I am glad you have found it all right," he said, as I thanked him and put it in my purse. When I came home after doing the shopping I found my mother looking worried.

"The gendarmes were here this morning," she told me.

"Well, they haven't been here for a long time now. Looking for hoarded food, I suppose?"

"So they said; but from the way they went about their task it didn't seem to me that they were entirely interested in food."

"Did they mention my name?"

"Not directly, but it came up several times."

"There is nothing to worry about, mother."

Perhaps an hour later Bertha came to tell me that a big roughly dressed man had called at the back door, asking if my letter for Mademoiselle Van Eurne was ready? I had never heard of Mademoiselle Van Eurne and was puzzled. The man I found waiting at the door was a complete stranger to me. He was dressed roughly enough, but somehow he carried the appearance of anything but a toiler. His Flemish was entirely fluent but held a harsh tone, which faintly suggested a German accent.

"Monsieur, I think you have made some mistake. You have been directed to the wrong house perhaps. I do not know who Madame Van Eurne is."

"Think carefully, Mademoiselle, you can trust me," he murmured.

"I have no idea what you are talking about. I dare say Monsieur Molendorp in the shop over there would know of the Van Eurnes."

I thought I caught a look of disappointment on his face, but he went with a muttered apology. I left the kitchen feeling vaguely frightened. I was certain the man was a German, but why was he trying to test me? I told myself that he had probably been detailed to do this throughout the town, in hopes some one might give themselves away, and that there was no cause for anxiety. At three o'clock a girl friend, Agnes Verbrey, hurried in with an agitated look. Detectives had just left her house after closely questioning every member of the family as to what they knew about myself. I could not understand it; then the thought that the matron at the hospital might perhaps spread some tale about me brought with it a little comfort.

Deepening shadows had begun to close on the room. It was the part of the day when the café was quiet. But suddenly a sound came from the front room: a sound that sent shivering fears through my heart. I was used to hearing rifle-butts clattering on the boards of the café as their owners dropped them carelessly in a corner, but this was different. It was the clean-cut crack made by rifle-butts when they met the ground from the slope to the attention—and in our café. I composed my features as best I could, and went to meet whatever terror awaited me. Standing in the café was an officer of the Brigade Staff and two soldiers with a Gefreiter in full marching order with fixed bayonets.

"To what reason are we indebted for this second intrusion to-day?" I asked, as calmly and quietly as I could make myself. The officer did not bother to salute.

"I have orders to make a thorough search of these premises, Fräulein," he said roughly. "Gefreiter," he went on, "you will place your men so that no one can leave or enter while we are here, then come with me." Looking again at me he began: "Fräulein, please hand me all your keys, it will save time and also," he added with a hard little smile, "your property."

"A search will yield you nothing, Herr," I assured him. "I have nothing to be afraid of, and I hope in future you will leave me in peace." He bowed when I handed him the keys and forthwith descended to the cellar with the

Gefreiter, for that was where the search was to begin. I was ordered to wait in the back parlour. Both my mother and father were out. From the noises that reached me I could tell that the search was of the most ruthless character, walls being tapped and every receptable being ransacked.

We can all look back to some moment in our lives, or some glaring oversight, and hardly believe ourselves capable of committing such a *faux pas*. Such human failings are apt to alter the whole course of our lives. I cannot for the life of me account for the neglect, unless it was due to the fact that I had become so accustomed to depend on myself doing the obvious right thing at the right moment, but even as I heard the two men mounting the stairs, it flashed on my brain with a sickening sense of horror that that very morning I had placed two tiny scrolls of code message under a strip of loose wallpaper behind the wash-stand in my bedroom. I had expected the drayman to call that day. Bertha, who had been upstairs, crept in, looking frightened, and told me that they were ripping open the mattresses and sorting the stuffing. The heavy footsteps upstairs seemed to wander from side to side of the room interminably, the suspense became unbearable. I waited white-faced and motionless, hoping against hope that after searching in the mattresses they would be satisfied.

Suddenly the noise upstairs stopped. Then hurried footsteps scurried across the room, and I heard them thundering down the stairs. The officer burst in. His whole demeanour had changed. With an air of savage, bullying triumph, he ground out:

"You see what I have found behind the washstand, Fräulein. You will come with me immediately to the Kommandant's office, where you will be formally charged. We have enough evidence now to put you in front of a firing squad any time we please.—Gefreiter, call the two men."

Bertha burst out weeping; but, now that the worst had happened, I was fiercely determined to keep my head, notwithstanding the numbing horror of this crushing turn of events.

Presently I was marching through the streets, bareheaded, between my guards with the officer in front and the Gefreiter in the rear. The rumour quickly spread, and men and women came running to watch us pass. "Knubs" congregated outside their billets swore and spat on the ground. At the Town-Kommandant's office I was formally charged as a spy, although the detailed charges were not specified, and I was not allowed to speak a word myself. To reach the prison our little party had to pass the tram terminus. As we approached a tram arrived, discharging crowds of rough and ready civilian labourers who were employed on making concrete dugouts in the German reserve line. A growl of disapproval and sympathy swept through the crowd of pushing, jostling humanity. I thought an attempt at rescue, which would have been worse than useless, might be made, but the escort marched quickly and steadily with set faces.

Somewhere behind me a man shouted: "Courage, little sister!" and it came to me as in a dream. We met a body of troops on their way to pack themselves into the cars of "Ça-na-fait-rien" to be rattled up front. They were singing with cheerful faces. All knew that certain of their number would never return to Roulers, and that others would return on stretchers, but why worry?—every one stood an equal chance of pulling through, and anyway, you didn't know what was going to happen to you until it did happen. I was not so lucky as they. I knew what was going to happen to me. There could be no doubt about that. A firing party in the dawn.

We reached the military prison; old Feldwebel Richter stood at the door, his tunic unbuttoned, smoking his curly Bavarian pipe. He took it from his mouth and stared in amazement. The light of pity showed in his eyes, then they hardened in bestial resentment—so friend Fräulein Cnockaert was a spy; then I saw pity again. He wiped his moustache, sprang to attention and saluted, then preceded us silently into the prison. A cell door clashed to and the drum of military boots receded down that corridor.

I sat down on my coarse bed. This was the end of my spying—a firing party in the dawn.—I heard their heels crash to attention, I heard the rattle as the rifles went up. I could not think how they had detected me—but what did it matter?—I had served my country to the best of my ability—and the Germans—I had done my duty by them, too—they could not deny that—but what did that matter?—what did that matter?—"If you are caught, it will probably be your own fault!"—"It will probably be your own fault!" The sound of a sentry pacing in the corridor came to me, slow, steady paces. It was cold and lonely and dark.—A firing party in the dawn.—I burst into tears.

CHAPTER XI

A shaft of wintry sunlight striking on my face through the cell window awoke me the next morning. I did not know where I was at first. Then I heard the sentry outside, and I was filled with sweating terror. For an hour I lay there perfectly motionless. Then I rose unsteadily in a sort of daze and dressed myself. After that I sat staring aimlessly at the opposite wall. The morning must have been well advanced, but still nobody came to the cell. At last the small trap in the door clicked back, and I heard two voices in conversation. The face of a detective, whom I had seen once or twice before, peered in at me and nodded. The panel slammed. A few minutes later the guard opened the door, set down a mug of tea and a tin plate with a fair-sized piece of black bread, and went out, relocking it. I swallowed the food automatically.

That went on for three days. Nobody spoke to me, nobody but the guard visited me. The only sound that reached me was the sound of their pacing, or the scraping and rattling when they relieved each other. In the morning came the tea and black bread; at midday a bowl of thick soup; and at night thinner soup with potatoes. Several times during daylight, and hourly during the night the panel in the door slid back and the guard examined me. My mind was almost a blank. I used to lie during the darkness waiting for the noise of the panel and the flash of the torch, counting the dreary hours to myself.

On the fourth morning I stirred out of a troubled doze to find all my senses as clear as a bell. I began to think furiously. I could see no hope for myself, but I determined that I would give them no help in dealing with my case. I had no idea how much they knew about my activities of the last two years. Were the wrist-watch and the notes the only things they had against me? Above all, I must not be led into disclosing those who had worked with me, for I was certain they would try by some means to drag everything out of me. Starvation seemed better than shooting. I would hunger strike from then on and end things that way.

During the afternoon the detective came to my cell who had previously peered at me through the panel. He was a big man with a long chin and a hideous twisted kink across the bridge of his nose, where something must have hit him very hard.

"You are going to die in a day or two," was the pleasant beginning. "So you may as well tell me the truth. We have your friends and they have confessed your complicity." He stood glaring down at me.

I knew the man was lying and kept silent. For half an hour he tried every means to trap me into an admission, even threatening to arrest my mother. Then he lost patience.

"Come on," he bawled, shaking his fist in my face. "I'll have it out of you if I kill you doing it. Who were the people who were employed in this business with you?"

I shook my head and with trembling knees sat down on the bed. A second later he hauled me to my feet, thrusting his face close into mine.

"Are you going to tell me—or shall I have to resort to— other measures?" he mouthed. "We have ways of making people speak, especially women." Then like the flash from a gun: "Who were those notes for? What do they say?"

Still I refused to say a word, and with that he left me, stamping out and slamming the door. This was Third Degree with a vengeance. Nor from then on was I allowed a moment of peace. That night he burst in no less than twenty times, storming, cursing, threatening. Day followed day and I ate no food. The food placed in my cell now was of a better quality, better probably than I could have procured outside in those scarce times, better than my guard ever had to eat. But I refused to be tempted by the savoury odour. The soldiers looked sorry for me when they removed the untouched food, and yet there was a gleam of satisfaction in their eyes, for it meant a first-class dinner for them. Three times each day and many times each night that terrible detective descended upon me like a vulture.

Sometimes, when he needed rest, another who was more quietly sinuous and persuasive in his methods took his place. Added to lack of food was lack of sleep. I could hardly keep my eyes open as first the one roared at me with bulging eyes and then the other whispered and hissed in my ear. I felt I should go mad with the horror of it all. The knowledge of one fact alone stood out to nerve me. My friends must be safe, for otherwise these detectives would never go to such lengths in trying to make me speak.

Then one whole day and one whole night passed and neither of them appeared. I concluded that they had sickened of the affair and given me up as a bad job. I was wrong. A woman was ushered into the cell, a Belgian, pretty, yet with an air that somehow repelled me.

"The military have employed me to look after you as wardress," she explained with a smile. "I want to help you all I can, my dear. I know this detective who is tormenting you well—a terrible fellow. Nothing turns him aside. Tell me in confidence what you know. We can keep back the vital information, but give me just enough to keep him quiet. I have some influence with him."

I stared hard at her. I had seen her before, and it was in company with the man she was talking about. She was probably his mistress.

"I am saying nothing," I replied. "I know nothing of spies who were working against the Germans in this town. They cannot do any good by tormenting me, and before long I shall have starved to death in any case."

"Do you realize that if you tell what you know you will be allowed to walk out of this prison a free woman," she whispered.

"Go back to your man," I cried weakly, "and tell him I'll see him in Hell before I say one word to him."

She grew crimson and spat on the ground.

"You bitch," she snarled. "You'll get what is coming to you, right enough."

"At any rate, I am not a traitor to my country," I said.

Then she rushed out, ordering the guard to bolt the door, and I lay back on my bed. I do not remember very clearly what happened after that. There followed one awful twenty-four hours throughout the whole of which one or other of my examiners sat by the bedside and plied me with fruitless questions. I became semi-unconscious. A military doctor whom I did not know came to see me the next day. I was still wearing the same clothes as when imprisoned three weeks earlier, but he allowed me clean linen and a piece of soap. No serious effort had been made to clean out the cell since I had been in it, and he ordered this to be done. He told me that if I refused to eat he would have me forcibly fed, and that it would be impossible to resist. I agreed, therefore, to eat a little. But cold, hunger, dirt and worry had undermined my strength, and during the next fortnight I grew worse daily. One morning two soldiers came in and lifted me on to a stretcher. I was taken to the civilian hospital of the Brothers Redemtoriste, but still as a military prisoner. Here the sisters were distinctly unfriendly, since they imagined I was a woman of low moral character.

Two days later I was informed that I was to be allowed to see my mother by the German Gefreiter who was in charge of me. I had taken more food and was feeling better, but for all that my mother told me that at first she did not recognize me. She had brought fruit and eggs for me. At first she wept, moaning: "My three sons have gone. And now they must take my daughter, too." I took her hand, but it was not necessary for me to tell her that what had to be, had to be. In a moment she had recovered herself and was telling me all the news of the place. Alphonse and Stephan sent kind messages, and what nerved me more than anything else was their assurance that they were "carrying on." They had told my mother that there were many at the hospital who were sorry for my plight, and that the surgeons intended to put in a good word for me at the forthcoming court martial. The twenty minutes that my mother was allowed with me had gone in a flash. The guard entered with impassive face and tapped her on the shoulder. My mother squeezed my hand so that I felt the bones of my fingers would snap. Then she went out with a brave face.

It was only when my mother came that the priests and sisters learnt the true state of affairs in regard to myself.

"It was a natural mistake," said the head sister, in explanation of their previous attitude. "Since you have done so much for Belgium it will be an honour to do all we can for you."

During the daytime I was locked in my room with a guard outside, but at night the military left, making the hospital authorities responsible for me. Then the priests and sisters would come and talk to me. Five weeks drifted by. With the best food they could procure I soon became well again. It seemed strange to think that I was waiting for death. Each day I hoped that my mother would come again, but in vain. At last, I asked the sentry outside the door if my mother could be asked to come. He said it had been strictly forbidden for anybody from the town to see me since her visit. Thinking it over afterwards, I felt it was better that our final parting should have occurred when neither of us realized that this was so. Then late one afternoon the Gefreiter came into the room.

"An ambulance will be waiting outside at seven o'clock tomorrow morning," he said. "You will be ready. You are going to Ghent."

~

We drew up outside the great grey military prison at Ghent. The Gefreiter handed me over to a middle-aged wardress whose face seemed made of wood. Here was the very essence of gloom. It was one step nearer the end, I told myself. It seemed to me that all the light had gone out of the world, but I was not sure that I cared now. The cell I was put in was better than the one at Roulers. There was something hard, cruel and threatening in its utter cleanliness. After several days one began to feel one was hardly human.

On the fourth day a lieutenant was shown into the cell, and the door was locked behind him. He held some papers in his hand. I rose, staring in his face.

"Sit down, Mademoiselle," he said quietly, and then after a pause: "By order of the General Officer Commanding Occupied Areas you will be tried by General Court-Martial in one week's time. In conjunction with the special decree recently issued, you are arraigned under Article 90 of the Military Penal Code, Sections 2 and 4, which concern respectively the destruction of munitions, and serving as a spy to the enemy."

He handed me a paper on which all the details had been written in French.

"I have been detailed to act in your interest as your defending officer, Mademoiselle," he went on.

"I do not wish for a defending officer."

"You do not trust me. You think that I should go to the authorities with what you would confide in me. You need have no fear of that. However, if you prefer, Mademoiselle, I can procure a civilian advocate of your own nationality for you."

"I have no reason to mistrust you, Herr Lieutenant. It is merely a matter of prudence. Besides, I do not believe that you could help my case. As for a civilian advocate, he would be worse than useless in the present circumstances."

"You will conduct your own defence?"

"I shall refuse to plead. I have not decided as yet whether I shall speak at all."

"I am not sure that you may not be wise, Mademoiselle," he said thoughtfully. "I understand that you have a most excellent character from the Roulers hospital authorities, which no doubt will be considered by the Court in dealing with your case. But do not pin too much faith on that. On the evidence which is held against you, it is my frank opinion that you are damned."

"I am only partially aware what the evidence is which the Prosecution does hold against me, and how it came to be obtained?"

"Well, I will tell you about that.—The events which led up to your arrest were these. A number of children in Roulers were seen one day by a passing soldier to be playing round a hole in the ground which they had discovered. It was upon the site of a supply dump which had recently gone up in flames under mysterious circumstances. This hole, apparently, had been disguised by a specially contrived lid. Below was a stone-paved shaft, which was found to lead to the Roulers Hospital, where there was another concealed exit. A gold wrist-watch was picked up. Since it bore the same initials as a nurse in the hospital, namely yourself, suspicion fell upon you, but it was quite possible that the watch might have belonged to somebody else. You know yourself what steps the authorities took to ascertain the ownership of that watch."

I nodded, and he called to the wardress to unlock the door.

"As you do not consider that I can be of use, Mademoiselle, I shall go. Should, however, you change your mind, I am always at your service."

"Thank you, Herr Lieutenant, it is a change to find someone who is kind."

"Whatever you did, I believe that you did it for the good of your country. Mademoiselle, may luck be with you." He bowed and clicked his heels. The wardress relocked the door after him, and I was alone.

I do not remember much about that week before the court-martial. I was an automaton. I think my brain hardly functioned.

CHAPTER XII

There is but one fate for a spy! That is Death!!"

That was the only consolation offered me by the grim-faced wardress when she brought me my black bread and tea on the Thursday morning of the court-martial. I awoke, glad to get the whole grim business over. I knew the trial would be a farce, that I would be condemned was certain. So if I was to be shot let it be quickly, without too much time' to think! It was about ten o'clock when there came a tramp of feet from the stone-flagged passage. The door of my cell swung back with a crash.

"The Fräulein will come."

A German Unter-Offizier stood stiffly to attention, and behind him I glimpsed two files of privates; their eyes stared ahead of them, inhuman and animal-like, without a vestige of interest. To them I was Convict Number So-and-so—a convicted spy—and they would aim their rifles at my heart with the same lack of interest. With a curt word of command and the ring of iron on the stones, I was surrounded, marched forward to meet my accusers. In the rear came a wardress who was to stand behind me during the trial.

At such times one notices little things: the smoke spiral wafting from a chimney, blown here and there by the wind; the sparrow perched arrogantly upon the iron gutter below the roof tiles. Then we were passing up some stone steps, through a passage, and in a moment I was facing eight officers seated at a long table, in the midst of whom was a ninth, the President. In front of each lay pens, sheaves of papers, and legal-looking books. Everything was most severe. I glanced at my judges. They were all scrupulously dressed as if about to go on parade. Most of them were of high rank, but I was struck by the youth of two very junior officers, one of whom wore an eyeglass. Two other officers were seated about five paces from the long table. As curt words of command sounded behind me, and the sound of the retreating footsteps of the guard was heard, one of these two officers rose. The farce opened. He was the Prosecutor. For a long while I listened to his voice as though in a dream. It all seemed so unreal. I could not even now believe I was being tried for my life.

The Prosecutor was a short, wiry individual, with steely grey eyes and a face devoid of pity or emotion. He marshalled his facts with cold insistent skill, and only twice did his eyes gleam with suppressed passion—once when accusing me of being the cause of the death of hundreds of his comrades-in-arms, and then at the end, when demanding that the Council send me to death! He was saying:

—"Martha Cnockaert, a Belgian subject, but nevertheless, under the jurisdiction of the Imperial German Government, is accused of offences against the German Military Code. German nationals, and quite rightly foreign nationals also, are subject to these laws. The offence is treason and is punishable by death!"

He paused. The only sound was a rustle of papers and a sharp intake of breath from one of the junior officers at the table.

I looked round. Not a vestige of pity or of mercy graced the whole Council, and strangely enough, only the white-haired old General, the President, with his clear-cut features and bemedalled tunic, appeared real.

"I will prove conclusively the guilt of the accused," continued the passionate voice. "The dangerous rôle she undertook was under the cloak of ministering angel, for to further her diabolical schemes she caused herself to be employed in a military hospital at Roulers. What better shield than this? A work of mercy! Who was less likely to fall under suspicion? But always, mark you, she was working near the Front. The Front where the latest and most vital information would manifest itself. After leaving her home village of Westroosebeke, she, knowing the enormous advantage of holding a military rendezvous, caused her parents to become the proprietors of the Café Carillon in Roulers. Coupled with the rôle of ministering angel, what better place could be chosen by a woman of charm and ability than this, for the gathering and dissemination of military information? Men will speak and boast of secrets in such surroundings. There is no doubt that she has been a dangerous and relentless enemy spy, from the first days, and is the undoubted cause of the deaths of hundreds of men—men who are our comrades-in-arms! Wireless code messages flashed from a nearby Neutral State have been intercepted and decoded. It was stated that the author or source of the information was 'L.' The very initial as is signed on the notes discovered in the accused's bedroom! While she has been astute enough not to sign any statement while in prison, she has at all times refused to speak of the destination of the notes."

He paused impressively.

"She dare not! But I will call witnesses who will testify to her confession of blood-guilt. These are times of stress and danger; the State and the lives of our comrades fighting the good fight in the trenches must be safeguarded, and no sentiment of sex or of womanhood must be allowed to blind our judgment. There is only one fate for the assassin who stands before this Council of Justice, and that, I demand in the name of our common Fatherland, is DEATH!!"

There was a deathly silence in the room as he sat down. The President glanced down at his papers, then looking up at me, said:

"These are most serious charges, Fräulein Martha Cnockaert. What answers have you?"

"I have nothing to say," I replied in Flemish; for throughout I refused to speak in German.

"Who were your associates in this work of passing military information to the enemy?—With whom did you work in Roulers?—Is it a fact that you worked with a known and recognized spy, Lucelle Deldonck?——"

To each of these questions I shook my head.

"Come," he said. "You are only injuring your own case. Try to be frank with the Court." Glancing down again at his papers and again fixing his eyes on my face, he asked. "Can you throw any light on those decoded wireless messages, or the author who is 'L.' Are you 'L'?"

I remained silent. Glancing over to the Prosecutor, he said:

"We will proceed with the evidence." The officer who sat with the Prosecutor rose and announced "Lieutenant Gustave Wolf." The officer from Brigade Headquarters who had arrested me, stepped into the room. The Prosecutor arose and after asking him to identify me, told him to detail to the Council the events leading up to my arrest.

"I am Brigade Headquarter Intelligence Officer, Roulers Area," he began. "Recently I was ordered to pay special attention to the matter that leakages of information were regularly passing over to the enemy from this district. The first clue I obtained was when over a period of several weeks we intercepted certain code messages. The bearers refused to speak. When decoded, these proved to be signed with the letter 'L.' I thought at first that these must have come from a woman, and a known enemy agent, Lucelle Deldonck, whose present whereabouts could not be traced, but whose name was entered in our files as dangerous. I thereupon caused test decoy messages to be sent. The result of this was that I became satisfied that the sender could not have been Lucelle Deldonck.

"My next step was to search the old reports regarding the Lucelle Deldonck affair for information about her friends. I found that Martha Cnockaert, who was working in the German Hospital, appeared to have been associated with her, although there was no direct evidence against her, and her conduct had been favourably reported upon by the authorities. The intercepting of the messages signed 'L' took place about midsummer of this year. Nothing further accrued and I was able to find no evidence that Martha Cnockaert was the mysterious 'L.'

"Then on the 25th of November of this year it was reported to me by a soldier that when passing across a piece of ground in the town where an important supply dump had only a month previously been destroyed by explosions, causing a fire—the subsequent Court of Enquiry were able to find no reasons for these explosions—he noticed some Belgian children playing around a hole in the ground. This hole had a cleverly camouflaged lid and had been accidentally discovered by the children. Upon examination I found that this led into an underground passage, and it had obviously been made through the roof of the passage to give some person or persons egress to the site of the dump. From the elaborate nature of the work which had been necessary for this purpose, from the jumble of footmarks in the dust on the floor of the passage and from the finding of a sack of tools which had been dropped, I judged that more than one person was concerned. Another exit to this passage, also apparently made recently, was found beneath a wooden hut in the Hospital grounds, which lie outside the town. This naturally turned my attention to the staff at the Hospital. Martha Cnockaert, being a Belgian, was obviously the most suspicious character, but I was assured by the Oberartz at the Hospital that she was above suspicion. She had recently been let off work at the Hospital, but was still there at the time the dump was destroyed.

"It was just after I had left the Hospital that my Gefreiter came to me with a gold wrist-watch which he had picked up in a corner of the passage near the dump opening. I found that it bore the initials M.C., which might stand for Martha Cnockaert. It occurred to me that the owner of the watch, realizing that it had been lost in a compromising spot, might be reluctant to reclaim it, and this, of course, was essential for my case. With the connivance of the Town-Kommandant, I prepared a little ruse, which is of no importance to this Court, but which in forty-eight hours had the desired result of bringing the owner, apparently quite unsuspicious, to claim her property. It was Martha Cnockaert. Late in the day I proceeded to her house and conducted a thorough search of the whole premises. In the bedroom of the accused, concealed in a loose strip of wallpaper behind the washing-stand, I found the two code messages the Court has before it. The code signature beneath these represents the letter 'L,' and is the same as on those messages I intercepted during the summer. I knew, therefore, that I had the right person."

The Prosecutor arose and asked:

"What was her demeanour upon being arrested?"

"She did not deny my accusation. As a matter of fact she assented to my charges, although I got no direct admission."

The President said: "I thank you, Herr Lieutenant."

The officer stood back, saluted and left the court-room.

The soldier who had discovered the hole on the site of the dump, the Gefreiter who had discovered the wrist-watch, and another Gefreiter who had heard me claim it in the Town-Kommandant's office, followed immediately with their evidence. Then there was a pause and a rustling of papers as the Court whispered among themselves, and my two code messages found in the bedroom passed from hand to hand.

The President looked up at me.

"Are these notes in your handwriting," he put quietly, clasping and unclasping his fingers.

I refused to answer. He nodded towards the Prosecutor, and again that officer beside him arose.

"Hauptmann Max Blathner," he announced. The horrible Third Degree examiner who had made my life a hell in Roulers prison entered the room. My whole being stiffened in protest on glimpsing my tormentor. He was dressed in spruce military uniform. The same farce was gone through. The Prosecutor arose and flung terse questions at him, and in return he addressed the Council.

"The prisoner more than once admitted to me that she was in the pay of the enemy!"

My whole soul revolted against the scoundrel's bare-faced perjury. Suddenly I found myself leaning forward, while a guard laid a hand on my arm.

"It is a lie," I said quietly. "This man tried by every human means to get me to commit myself. He invaded my privacy night and day at Roulers prison—when I was weak from hunger and loss of sleep he manhandled me, threw me against the walls, swore that he would drag the truth from me or kill me. And now you take that sort of evidence on oath!"

The President held up his hand.

"There is no need to interrupt," he remarked. "You are being charged on specific charges. If they are disproved you will be released."

"But," I insisted, "if you take this man's evidence, why not call the Belgian woman who is his mistress and whom he sent to me as an 'agent provocateur' in prison?" There was an ill-concealed smile on the faces of the officers present, but the President frowned. The witness grew scarlet in the face and cast a vindictive look in my direction. The wardress came forward and laid a hand on my shoulder.

"That is neither here nor there," muttered the President into his white moustache. We are concerned only with the facts. Proceed with your evidence." He turned to the examiner, who drew himself stiffly up and gave a highly garbled version of his interviews with me in my cell. He said:

"It wasn't so much that I attempted to get her to sign a statement as to her guilt—that we knew—but to get at the fountain-head, and her associates in this conspiracy. She refused at all times to divulge who her accomplices were."

I felt and knew his word would be taken before mine. Then the President was speaking again as if from a great distance. He had to repeat his words before I could grasp their sense.

"Have you anything further to say?"

I stared at him, at the circle of faces now not only hostile but grim and determined. But, in spite of my resolution to say nothing, in face of evidence so patently manufactured, I was unable to stem the flow of indignant protests which welled from my distracted heart.

"Of what use is it for me to speak?" I cried, giving way to pent-up emotion. "You have been offered proof of my guilt on the testimony of a man like this. . . . I well know that I was condemned before I ever walked into this room to take my part in this solemn farce. I do not recognize this Court or its verdict. If you think that the mailed might of Germany can keep down the spirit of the oppressed Belgium nation you are mistaken. You will have to arrest, imprison and murder every man, woman and child born with the spirit of freedom in Belgium. I look on myself," I continued passionately, "as a soldier in the field, with an ordinary combatant's rights, in face of an invader who has committed pillages and rapine, and who has made laws to suit his own convenience. You are Germans, I am Belgian; you the oppressors, I the oppressed; so in my own country it is perfectly legitimate for me to use every weapon in my power to defeat such an abhorrent machine which is attempting to overrun our beloved land. Although this trial has been kept as secret as the grave itself, you must not think my death will pass unnoticed, for as sure as the sun rises to-morrow, so will my death be avenged a thousand times over!"

"Vive la Belgique! Vive les Alliés!"

There was a chorus of ejaculations from the Court and the President half rose to his feet. A guard was gripping me tight by either arm, when I saw the aged President look with some little surprise at an Unter-Offizier, who came stiffly to attention in front of the Council table. He handed a note to the President, saluted and retired. The President signed to the Prosecutor, who rose and respectfully listened to the President. The white-haired old man seemed to be at a loss. He called over the officer who during the proceedings had been sitting with the Prosecutor, and, conferring together with two senior officers at the table, they evidently came to some decision. The Prosecutor and his companion moved back, and immediately the announcer, who I suppose was acting as clerk of the Court, said:

"Herr Doctor Herbert Stolz.—The Court have decided to hear his evidence for the defence."

The keen-faced Oberartz from the Roulers Hospital came silently into the room. After being sworn the President informed him that it was very much against the usual procedure, but that after conferring together, the Court had decided to hear the evidence of the Oberartz.

"I am Oberartz at the Roulers Military Hospital. The accused has worked untiringly and unsparingly under my command for many anxious months, and has always shown great attention and a merciful bearing in her work. I have come here voluntarily to testify to her good character, and her ceaseless endeavours to alleviate the sufferings of our wounded countrymen."

The Prosecutor arose and questioned the Oberartz.

"Would it surprise you to know that the accused has confessed to her guilt?"

"The guilt or the innocence of the accused as proved by this Court does not concern me."

"Does it not strike you that the accused obtained the job of a nurse in a German hospital solely for the purpose of carrying on espionage against us?"

"The accused may have acted as a spy in the interests of her country. After all, you have been fighting in the interests of your country. But, knowing the accused as I do know her, I believe that she worked as a nurse purely in the interests of humanity. I know that the surgeons under my command at the Roulers Hospital, who came in daily contact with Fräulein Cnockaert, will agree with me in my attitude."

"How long did she work under your direct supervision ?"

"The whole of the period she was engaged at the hospital, and at all times her work was voluntary."

The Prosecutor, glancing over to the table with a sly meaning look, said:

"Then you will no doubt tell the Court that you saw a very great deal of this engaging voluntary Fräulein ?"

"You would insinuate that I am in love with the accused?" he asked quietly. "That is absolutely untrue. The whole of my specialist career has been spent in conjunction with staffs of ladies and nurses. My professional career is open to the scrutiny of this or any other tribunal," he said quietly. "And, in addition, I am a most happily married man with a large family. I am actuated by my sense of justice, purely and simply." Turning to the President, he addressed him in a firm voice. "My principal object in coming here was to inform the court that Mademoiselle Martha Cnockaert was awarded the highest honour that our Fatherland can bestow.—For her services as a nurse, during which she risked her life in the field, she was specially recommended to His Royal Highness, the Duke of Würtemberg, and was subsequently a recipient of the Iron Cross."

A profound impression seemed to have been made on the Court. Two other doctors from the Roulers Hospital followed the Oberartz. In each instance the Prosecutor followed the same lines as practised on the Oberartz, but they just as easily refuted his vile insinuations. After anxiously conferring with two senior officers at the table, the President rose and addressed the Court.

"Sentence will be promulgated in four days. Remove the prisoner, and clear the Court," he ordered.

The German wardress told me I had been a fool not to admit everything and throw myself on the mercy of the Court.

"You must not think the intervention of the Oberartz can help you."—Throw myself on the mercy of such a Court! From their faces not one iota of pity had shown itself during the whole proceedings. The only ray of sunshine had been the friendly faces of the Roulers doctors. For their forlorn mission my heart welled with gratitude. And now here I was enclosed by the too-familiar cell walls, awaiting those few curt words which would bring me face-to-face with a firing squad. Perhaps those last four days of waiting were the worst; awaiting promulgation of the sentence. They were purgatory. Each morning I looked at the sun through the bars. Maybe only forty-eight hours to live? Next morning only twenty-four?

Yet I ate, I slept, I moved; a human creature so soon to be put secretly out of sight under clay sodden by winter rains. My mother would miss me terribly, and where was Lucelle Deldonck; she who had given me my chance to serve my country and who by now was probably occupying an unnamed and unhonoured grave? I thought of "Joan the Maid," and prayed to her for strength to support me in my great suffering. Then at last a German officer arrived, accompanied by an

Unter-Offzier, and a file of men. The door clanged back to the ring and stamp of steel. The officer saluted with punctilious politeness.

"Prepare yourself, Fräulein," he said, "to hear the promulgation of your sentence. You will need courage!"

As in a dream I was marched into the same room that an eternity ago I was tried in. The President was sitting at a smaller table with two of the senior officers of the Council. Terse orders rang out behind me, and a deathly silence ensued. The President slowly arose, and taking up a paper, addressed me:

"It is a terrible thing to condemn a fellow-creature; especially when that creature is a woman; but you have been the cause of the deaths of many of my countrymen during the many months of your nefarious activities. The sentence is therefore that at an hour and place to be appointed later, you be taken out and shot to death!"

The Unter-Offizier, standing stiffly to attention, shouted so that the room rang:

"Judgment in the name of His Imperial Majesty! Present Arms!"

With a steady pace we marched back to the cells, and it seemed as though I was in another body, watching the receding figure of the woman prisoner between the grey-clad guards.

The tragic farce was played out!

CHAPTER XIII

I would fain draw a veil over the ensuing misery. It is an extraordinary thing to lie under sentence of death, yet during the short interval between promulgation of the sentence and its execution I do not remember experiencing much fear. Life was bounded by weeping dawns, the splash of raindrops of a dismal February, those scant coarse meals, and blessed sleep.

A special wardress had been assigned to me since I had been condemned. She moved in and out of my cell like a robot gargoyle, neither speaking, smiling nor showing she was indeed human. For her I was a number so soon to be put out of existence. I was not allowed to communicate with the outer world. A German priest, a kindly man, visited me, and I made my peace with God and man. Then, unexpectedly, the priest came to see me again.

"I do not want to raise any false hopes, my child," he said, "but I really think there is just a chance you may escape the death penalty."

I stared at him blankly. The idea had never crossed my mind. The faces of the President and the officers on that terrible morning had been as though graven from steel, grim and unrelenting. I could not envisage their superiors granting a reprieve. It was as though my mind had been frozen into stone. Now painfully it began to stir, to move, to think of possible "might be's."

"Steady," soothed the priest. "Calm yourself, child."

It needed all my will power to stop the insane laughter that bubbled to my lips. I found my fingers tearing the cuffs of the prison uniform. Presently after a few more kindly remarks he left, while I threw myself down on the bed and strove to make my mind a blank. Yet the priest had been right. It was a kindly thought to warn me, for if I had heard nothing of the reprieve till the official announcement, maybe I should have gone mad.

Next morning the old scenes were re-enacted, but this time with a new meaning. Again there came the stamp of feet, the clack of rifle-butts on the stone-flags. Bolts were shot back and the same officer faced me as he who had originally taken me before my judges. This time he threw me a smile.

"Please to come, Fräulein. The Court awaits."

Again that short passage up the stone steps, through the corridor, and into the room where only a day or so ago I had listened to nails being hammered into my coffin. This time there were but two officers, and my fears were quickly put at rest. In a formal tone the old President read over the charge and the sentence, though my heart stood still when he repeated the dread words that I was to be shot to death forthwith. Then he turned to me.

"Do you understand what I am saying?" he asked. "The Commander-in-Chief of Areas under Occupation has graciously consented to commute this death sentence into one of imprisonment for life. He has been guided in this by the fact that you had been awarded the Iron Cross for meritorious work in the field, and also owing to the special representations made on your behalf by the Authorities at Roulers. Have you anything you wish to say?"

I shook my head. At that moment I could not have uttered a word. Presently they led me from the courtroom. The thing was over and done with, yet I felt no great elation at having escaped a quick unknown grave. I was a prisoner for life! I began to reflect what that meant. God knew I should have enough time for reflection in the dreary years ahead. But then my whole being quickened. One day the Germans would be beaten. *They could not win*, and even if they found time to transport me to some grim fortress in the Fatherland, I was a political prisoner bound to be closely inquired for by the avenging Allies.

So I began an unending routine, an iron regime without soul or mercy, but buoyed up with the burning conviction that deliverance would come. Soon after dawn I was awakened, given a little tea substitute, and set to clean out my cell. Then came my breakfast, tea, and black sour bread made from God knew what. An empty stomach is said to stimulate the mind, but I was too utterly weary even to plan an attempt at escape. Our meals consisted mainly of beetroot and a thick soup made of beans, for the British blockade was strangling Central Europe. Mashed potato peelings were a luxury. Tea and coffee substitutes, and the abominable black sour bread were the rule, a strange diet on which I grew fat, but very weak. I have since heard it said that the Germans put camphor in our drink which caused the increase in weight.

Very rarely would the grim wardress throw me even a civil word. Each day I was given string and straw, and expected to make so much matting, unless I wished for disciplinary action to be taken against me, which meant still further curtailment of my meagre ration. The work was terribly fatiguing to eyes, brain and fingers. I began mat-making in a room with twenty-five other women inmates of the prison. I was not allowed to sit near them, and never did I get a chance of speaking one word to them. I used to see them at exercise in the yard, weary-eyed wretches, with drooping shoulders, who shuffled round in an eternal circle.

The weeks and months passed. I distinguished time from the position of the sun, season only from heat and cold. Always I was tormented with thoughts of my future. Bright hopes alternating with fits of deep depression. At times my soul cried out in bitter protest. "Oh God, how long? How long?"—Was this really to be the manner of my existence as long as I lived?

Then of a sudden I felt sick. It was the food and lack of fresh air.

"I do not like to see you like this," said my doctor friend from the Roulers Hospital. He had taken a great deal of trouble to get a special pass to see me, and to bring me a little extra food and some chocolate. He was deeply shocked at my appearance. Up to then he had been my only means of hearing about events happening in the great outside world. He told me sadly that the War *must* be soon finished. Humanity could not stand it long. Even if Germany did not win, he thought his country could force a draw. He had no doubt therefore that as a political prisoner I would be freed. In any case he promised if at all possible to keep acquainted with my movements, and he added:

"I will try and see the Governor about you. Maybe I can get you moved to a hospital." He failed, but not from want of trying.

The months slid endlessly by, a procession of empty days and nights. Stories of prisoners who tame rats and even spiders are true. I know it, because I made a rat my friend. At first he was shy, but within a month he would eat out of my hand. A friendly creature with beady eyes glancing in suspicion this way and that. When one day he did not come I wept helplessly. He had probably been killed as I never saw him again.

Still the soul-destroying routine went on. We are the legion of the lost, I thought. It hardly seemed possible for human nature to suffer so acutely. Years after—or so it seemed—I awakened one morning by the clashing of church bells. There was a murmur of excited voices in the yard where before there had only been silence, and a strange undefinable stir in the air. I judged the time long past the hour when the grim-faced wardress should visit me. Some spark of hope flickered in my brain, giving birth to a tiny flare of shivering excitement.

The shouts grew louder. The clamour of the bells had swollen into one perpetual mad jangle. Footsteps raced along the flagged corridor, bolts were shot back, and I saw half a dozen wild-eyed, dishevelled soldiers standing on the threshold.

"The War is ended!" they yelled. "You are free! free!" Then like a "Jack-in-the-box" they were gone, slamming the door behind them! I flew to it. No, the lock had snapped to. I was still a prisoner while the War was over!

Had Germany won? Were they in Paris? No, this could not be, reason told me. But it was maddening to know nothing, to surmise a thousand possible and impossible things. In despair, sobbing and weeping I banged feebly on the door and then sank down exhausted on the bed.

Within an hour the men returned, unlocking every door in the prison. Out we streamed, half-crazed men and women mingling with German infantry and marines. Everyone seemed running. No one appeared to carry rifles, but a crackling of rifle fire from one part of the town told of a stand being made.

All was chaos, soldiers and civilians running in every direction, groups dancing and shouting at the street corners, men mad-drunk looting the cafés and dragging the barrels of liquor into the road. Nobody took any notice of me in my ugly prison uniform. My one thought was to get away.—To hide! To hide! Anywhere! I ran aimlessly about the streets of Ghent, and then I found myself out in the open country, stumbling, falling, sobbing, babbling continually to myself as I went on and on. At first there were several others with me, then I was alone.

I heard shouts behind me in a strange language. Then I recognized English voices. Steel-helmeted men in khaki were advancing up the road behind me. I could see other parties moving in the fields upon either side. It was the British advance guard.

I turned and made towards them frantically. The mud-bespattered men paused in amazement as if they thought I was going to attack them. I tumbled into the arms of the nearest man, narrowly missing the point of his bayonet as he let his rifle fall. My brain was buzzing.

"An officer, an officer!" I wailed, and then everything went blank.

A corporal, with his helmet tipped well back off his grimy forehead was kneeling over me, splashing the contents of his water-bottle in my face when I opened my eyes. I was lying by the roadside. British troops were passing steadily, singing lustily as they went. A subaltern helped me to a sitting position.

"I belong to the British Secret Service," I murmured. "Two years ago I was captured. Since then I have been a prisoner.

I have no money, nothing—my parents live in Roulers. Can you help me to get there ?"

"You look as though a drink would do you good, Mademoiselle," he said, producing a whisky flask.

Presently I was being escorted back towards Ghent on the arm of the corporal.

"Well, Mademoiselle," he was saying. "This is the end of the War. But I reckon the people in this country will have a lot of cleaning up to do.—Come to think of it, I s'pose spying is about as unpleasant as being in the trenches, 'cept that yer gets more chances of 'avin' a wash."

"I feel as though I have just awakened out of a nightmare," I told him. "But at moments I'm still not quite sure whether I have woken up."

"That's exactly my sentiments, too!" he answered.

CHAPTER XIV

Great happiness can be as poignant as great suffering. In my first days of freedom my heart was almost suffocated with happiness. The sound of Belgian voices was the sweetest I had ever heard. I was at last safe among friends. The British passed me on to the headquarters of a French regiment in Ghent, and telephone messages were sent through to Roulers. Within a few hours a *tres galant* French officer had put me on a returning lorry. I had to pinch myself very hard to realize it was not all a heavenly dream. I do not remember a second of that journey for the tears of happiness that welled to my eyes.

The lorry drew up before the battered, crumbling front of the Café Carillon. What a change had come over Roulers. The town had been comparatively little damaged when I had left it in 1916. Now there was hardly a house with a roof to it. The air of desolation was ghastly. In place of the old field-grey figures which had haunted the streets were the sky-blue uniforms of France and the khaki of American "doughboys." Nearly all of the fifty inhabitants of Roulers who had stayed sheltering in the cellars till the bitter end, were gathered uproariously at the door to greet me. It was with the utmost difficulty that I could make my way through them to my mother, who was too upset to meet me outside.

"Thank God," she murmured, crying and laughing at the same time. "We heard a thousand rumours—that you had been shot—deported to Germany—died in prison."

Then I learned what seemed a veritable miracle. All my brothers had come through with their lives, although the two youngest would be permanent invalids. Within a week Lucelle had joined us, a little older, a little more weary-looking, but with the same unquenchable spirit.

"Those were the bad times, eh?" she chuckled. "More than six times I gave myself up as done for. Yes—Holland was a good place in those days when one had the 'Vampires' behind with their noses to the ground——"

Every day brought us fresh surprises; friends turning up who had been long mourned as lost, people who had escaped by miracles. How we talked—of "Canteen Ma," of the kindly Oberartz, of No. 63, of poor Fashugel, of "Silent Willy," of Alphonse, who was soon to become a priest, and all those others, friend and foe, who have passed across these pages. Ah, happy days. Home again—to see the Town-Kommandant's office a deserted ruin across the Place; to see good-natured Belgian gendarmes in the streets; to walk at one's will in the town, day or night, without the thought of the accursed curfew; to hear no longer those eternal guttural voices, to know that those happy days of before the War were coming back, even though we did live in a land of ruins.

The French and American soldiers in the town did all they could to help us. Everyone belonged to one great family. Old inhabitants poured back into the town. They came by rail and they came by road, with their donkey-carts and their packs on their backs. Many were helped on their way in Allied lorries and ambulances, and old women found their bundles being carried by strange grinning soldiers, who did not understand a word they said. Families stood gazing dismally upon the ruins of their homes, but a moment later they were cheerful and ready to sing. Mighty Germany was beaten to her knees! The dust clouds had subsided behind the last of the field-grey armies, the Areas under Occupation had become La Belgique, once again. But I, at any rate, shall always remember some of those nobler emissaries, men of all ranks, who came with grey wave.

It seemed at first as though we should never return to normal conditions, but as the months slipped by, beautiful new buildings began to spring up all over Flanders. All the time-worn architecture of the past was dust, but with amazing skill exact replicas were constructed everywhere. Prosperity returned to the land. Lack of food and exercise and constant anxiety had worn me to a shade of my former self, and for a long time I was an invalid in body, if not in mind. I could not bear the sight or smell of meat and good food, and I had to live on potato peeling and turnip soup. The prison routine seriously weakened my eyes and for some months I was under the care of doctors, as I almost went blind. My demobilization papers and my prison pay arrived from the British Intelligence Commission. I received an intimation that I had been mentioned in despatches by Sir Douglas Haig and that a British decoration was to be sent to me. I was honoured to receive the French and Belgian Legions d'Honneur, also.

Our old house at Westroosebeke was to be rebuilt, and I made a pilgrimage to the ruins where my father æons before had been nearly roasted alive. Hardly a brick stood one upon another. Only a notice on a bullet-marked board told the returning pilgrim "This is Westroosebeke." The leafy, whispering lanes and the smiling glades where we had

spent our childhood were a hideous pock-marked wilderness. Standing near the site of the Austrian telegraph hut I
wondered what had become of all the puppets of the drama.
A party of British soldiers were resting by the roadside, and a
young officer seeing me standing there came over and asked in
a quiet voice if I had once lived here. That young officer not
long afterwards became my husband. . . .

~

Not long after my marriage I happened to come to England
with my husband. He suggested that I should put in a claim at
the War Office for a refund of the money from my own pocket
which I had given British prisoners when helping them to escape,
as also other amounts which I had contributed to a secret fund
for the assistance of prisoners and small sums expended on odd
occasions. Altogether it amounted to a few hundreds of pounds,
which I had expended with a perfectly good will, but rightly or
wrongly would not be sorry to see again.

The courteous pleasant-faced man behind the big desk in
Whitehall, smiled at me as though I was a naughty little girl,
rested his elbows on the table and plaited his fingers.

"Quite, quite," he pronounced, when he had heard my
case. "But let me see—you have signed your demobilization
papers, have you not?"

I agreed, but explained that I understood that the papers
I had signed were dealing solely with my prison pay; a fact
which the Intelligence commissioners had assured me; and
adding that at the time when the transaction had gone through
I was not in a fit state of health to bother my head about such
questions. The courteous official rose elegantly and gazed at
the door, as much as to say: "Well, now it is time to go. . . ."

"I am afraid I can do nothing for you, Madame," was what he actually did say. "The act of signing those papers cancelled any official indebtedness on our part. I am sure you see my point."

"Then I have no hope of regaining my money," I put as a last resort.

"You see, Madame, there are no special funds to which I could apply for your claim. If I might suggest it—er—could you not go to the Germans?—Put in a special claim against the Reparations Commission."

I nearly laughed in his face.

I, who had risked death daily at the trigger fingers of a German firing party, who was responsible for the destruction of many German lives, who had been court martialled and condemned to death for espionage—I was to go to Berlin and demand payment for helping British prisoners to escape. He was a *farceur*, that man.

My husband took my arm.

"Don't bother about it," he said. "We have other things to think about." He was right. It was not worth bothering about. Red tape is red tape all the world over.

We went back to Flanders where the work of reconstruction was going on apace. In a year's time a new house stood on the site of our old house at Westroosebeke, and flowers as gay as the flowers of 1914 grew in a new garden.

So for me, in the end, the War brought happiness!

The Pool of London Press is a publisher inspired by the rich history and resonance of the stretch of the River Thames from London Bridge downriver to Greenwich. The Press is dedicated to the specialist fields of naval, maritime, military and exploration history in its many forms. The fine history of London and the Thames also features. The Press produces beautifully designed, commercial, non-fiction volumes and digital products of outstanding quality for a dedicated readership featuring strong narratives, magnificent illustrations and the finest photography.

A selection of titles from the Pool of London Press can be found on the following pages.

POOLOFLONDON
WWW.POOLOFLONDON.COM

THE COLD WAR SPY POCKET-MANUAL

The Official Field-manuals for Spycraft, Espionage and Counter-intelligence

Edited and compiled by Philip Parker

Some twenty-five years after its conclusion, yet with its echoes resonating once more in contemporary East-West relations, the rigors and detail of many aspects of the Cold War are becoming increasingly of interest. Furthermore, at the very same time many of the records of the period are beginning to become accessible for the first time. At the forefront of this unique conflict, that divided the world into two opposing camps for over four decades, were the security services and the agents of these secretive organizations.

The Cold War Spy Pocket-Manual presents a meticulously compiled selection of recently unclassified documents, field-manuals, briefing directives and intelligence primers that uncover the training and techniques required to function as a spy in the darkest periods of modern history. Material has been researched from the CIA, MI6, the KGB and the STASI. As insightful as any drama these documents detail, amongst many other things, the directives that informed nuclear espionage, assassinations, interrogations and the 'turning' and defection of agents.

- Full introduction and commentary provided by leading historian and former diplomat.

- Presents for the first time the insightful documents, many of which inspired Cold War novelists including John Le Carré, Len Deighton and Ian Fleming.

- Beautifully retro-styled and cloth-bound.

£8.99 • Hardback • 128 pages • ISBN 978-1-910860-02-1

THE LAST BIG GUN

At War & At Sea with HMS *Belfast*

Brian Lavery

As she lay in dry dock, devastatingly damaged by one of Hitler's newly deployed magnetic mines after barely two months in service, few could have predicted the illustrious career that lay ahead for the cruiser HMS *Belfast*. After three years of repairs to her broken keel, engine- and boiler-rooms, and extensive refitting, she would go on to play a critical role in the protection of the Arctic Convoys, would fire one of the opening shots at D-Day and continue supporting the Operation Overlord landings for five weeks.

Her service continued beyond the Second World War both in Korea and in the Far East before she commenced her life as one of the world's most celebrated preserved visitor ships in the Pool of London. Her crowning glory however came in December 1943 when, equipped with the latest radar technology, she was to play the leading role in the Battle of the North Cape sinking the feared German battlecruiser *Scharnhorst*, the bête-noir of the Royal Navy. In doing so the ship's crew made a vital contribution to, what was to be, the final big-gun head-to-head action to be fought at sea.

In *The Last Big Gun* Brian Lavery, the foremost historian of the Royal Navy, employs his trademark wide-ranging narrative style and uses the microcosm of the ship to tell the wider story of the naval war at sea and vividly portray the realities for all of life aboard a Second World War battleship.

- The illustrious survivor of the last big-gun head-to-head 'broadside' engagement at sea.

- The very first complete 'biography' of HMS *Belfast*.

- Exhaustively researched from primary sources and interviews and written in the matchless narrative style of the award-winning, *Sunday Times* bestselling author Brian Lavery.

£25.00 • Hardback • 376 pages • ISBN 978-1-910860-01-4

THE MAPMAKERS' WORLD

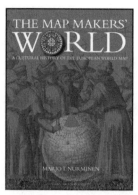

A Cultural History of the European World Map

Marjo T. Nurminen

The Mapmakers' World illuminates the fascinating cultural history of European world maps: what do historical world maps tell of us, of our perception of the world, and of places and peoples that are foreign to us? Who were the makers of these early world maps? How were the maps created and for whom were they drawn and printed? For what purposes were they used? What kind of information did they pass on? The answers to these questions open up a fascinating narrative of discovery and cartography relating not only to ideology and political power but also the histories of art and science.

- Lavishly illustrated history of the European world map.

- One thousand years of art, science, exploration, power and propaganda.

- Great illustrations of maps, paintings and artworks from the finest private and public collections as well as specially commissioned diagrams.

- The comprehensive history of European maps in one volume telling the exciting story of how cartographers first fully imaged the globe.

£50.00 • Hardback • 360 pages • ISBN 978-1-910860-00-7